MW00416573

With *Bulletproof Marriage*, Col. Grossman and Adam Davis provide precision guidance for sheepdogs on how to build resilient marriages. This is an essential guide for America's protectors to work on their most important relationship, which often suffers mightily while they serve us.

—**Mark Divine**, author of *The Way of the SEAL*, and founder of Sealfit and Unbeatable Mind

Marriage is not easy and being married to a sheepdog is not for the faint of heart. This book, along with your Bible, is a great tool to keep your marriage strong! This will bless many couples. Thank you for writing it.

—**Stephanie Rogish**, wife of a cop and author of the *Sheepdogs* kids book

A 90-DAY DEVOTIONAL

BULLETPROOF
MARRIAGE

Adam Davis and Lt. Col. Dave Grossman

BroadStreet Publishing® Group, LLC
Savage, Minnesota, USA
BroadStreetPublishing.com

Bulletproof Marriage: A 90-Day Devotional

978-1-4245-5759-2 (hardcover)
978-1-4245-5760-8 (e-book)

Stock or custom editions of BroadStreet Publishing titles may be purchased in bulk for educational, business, ministry, fundraising, or sales promotional use. For information, please email info@broadstreetpublishing.com.

Literary agent, Cyle Young, of the Hartline Literary Agency
Cover and interior design by Chris Garborg at garborgdesign.com
Typesetting by Kjell Garborg at garborgdesign.com

Printed in China
19 20 21 22 23 5 4 3 2 1

CONTENTS

Section Three: Conflict Resolution

Section Four: The Intimacy Initiative

Section Five: Affirming One Another

Section Six: Oneness

INTRODUCTION

This book is for all "sheepdogs" (by whom, in this context, we mean all first responders and military) and your spouses. Throughout your journey along this selfless path, you will face unimaginable challenges. Challenges most will never understand or experience. These circumstances can create a more unified commitment and bond between you and your spouse, or it can create an atmosphere of contention and strife.

If this is your first time hearing the phrase "sheepdog," it's important to understand the deeper meaning of this phrase.

The sheepdog is the one, guided by the Great Shepherd, who is willing to fight for, and at times even die for, other people's loved ones—the innocent sheep. The wolf is eager to kill, steal, and destroy, but only the sheepdog and the Great Shepherd love enough to die for the sake of all the sheep! Sometimes the greatest love is not sacrificing your life, but living a life of sacrifice. As a sheepdog, whether military or first responder, you have chosen a life of sacrifice. We store up our riches in heaven, but studying God's Word and following His path can provide us with amazing gifts of strength, peace, and wisdom. One of His greatest blessings can be found in your relationship with your spouse. Use this ninety-day devotional to grow closer to Christ and build a more resilient, bulletproof marriage.

One day the sheepdog will finally rest at the feet of the Great Shepherd, yearning to hear those words, "Well done, thou good and faithful servant" (Matthew 25:21 KJV).

As you move through this devotional, you will encounter relevant Scripture and daily devotions designed for you and your spouse. Many are real stories in which the names and identities have been changed. After each devotion is a quick tip summarizing the devotion for that day and practical action steps for you and your spouse. To complete the day's entry, you'll find a specific challenge for each of you, a few questions you can discuss together, and a prayer.

As you progress through this devotional, don't look at it as another book. It's a ninety-day challenge—a marriage boot camp—designed to help you make your marriage stronger and more resilient. There's more in this book than you can probably tackle in one pass. So just grab what you can this time around and let it be a resource God uses in your marriage for years to come.

Take ninety days to bulletproof your marriage and make it as great as it can be. Are you up for it?

Dave Grossman

Lt. Col., US Army (ret.)

Author and sheepdog

Foundation in Communication

Mission Impossible

Jesus looked at them intently and said, "Humanly speaking, it is impossible. But with God everything is possible."

MATTHEW 19:26 NLT

"Hey rookie, what are you doing in the patrol briefing room at this time of day?"

The pasty-looking sergeant wasn't really concerned with Robinson's reason for being there. He just wanted him gone from his presence.

"Hey sarge, I was wrapping up some paperwork and heading back out. About to meet my wife for lunch."

"You married? How long?" the sergeant asked.

"We've been married six years. Two kids."

Without wasting a breath, the sergeant replied, "I give it five more. Five years on this job and you'll be divorced. It's impossible for a cop to stay married with the crap we see every day. Good luck kid. You're gonna need it."

That conversation didn't quite hit the encouragement level

the newly sworn officer was looking for from a supervisor, but it was a clear wake-up call.

Everyone may tell you the alarming statistics regarding marriage, adultery, substance abuse, and suicide associated with your career in the military or as a first responder. But what they fail to mention is that nothing is impossible when you cultivate a daily, intimate relationship with God and place Him at the center of your life. That means your marriage *does* stand a fighting chance. That means your marriage has room to grow and thrive and you do *not* have to be a statistic. Get beneath the superficial, fluffy discussions that have no bearing or fruit. Go deep. Have meaningful conversations with your spouse and discuss the threats, discover solutions, and create practical steps to combat the challenges you will face in your marriage.

Quick Tip

It's time to decide who you will believe. Are you going to believe the voices who say your marriage will become a statistic, or will you believe what God's Word promises to those who are obedient and practice His truths? It's up to both spouses to go deep in your discussions. Don't let the dating years be the only lasting memory of meaningful conversation in your relationship.

Sheepdog

Think about the last conversation you had with your spouse. If that was your final conversation, would it be worth remembering? It's great to talk about family-related issues, but make an effort to sit down with your spouse, grab a cup of coffee or tea, read the Bible together, and talk about it. Learn from and challenge each other. Grow together spiritually. The longer you are together, the closer you will grow in your intimacy and the more richly blessed your life together will be.

Spouse

Take the first step into deep-diving discussions together. If this doesn't interest you, or if you have no desire to dig deep with your spouse and grow together, check your heart to see if you've allowed apathy to dominate your life. Find something that interests you both intellectually and spiritually and explore it together. These things will serve as a conduit of conversation between you and your spouse and help keep your lines of communication open and clear.

Questions for Discussion

- What are some things you would like to discover and explore with your spouse so that you can grow in intimacy?
- What is one simple way to implement biblical discussion and study in your marriage? Share your ideas.

Heavenly Father, we acknowledge your power as the Almighty Creator of all heaven and earth. You are the Creator, and you created us in your image. Help us awaken our desire to learn, grow wiser, and take this journey together as husband and wife. May this journey lead us into a deeper place of intimacy. Amen.

The Tone of Love

Let your conversation be always full of grace, seasoned
with salt, so that you may know how to answer everyone.

COLOSSIANS 4:6

A sheepdog holds the line, stands guard, confronts evil, and battles against the vilest enemies of society. Gradually, this often results in a tone of conversation at home that resembles the verbal commands on the battlefield. You might need to consider taking a moment or two before responding to your spouse, carefully considering your words and the tone of your voice. Think about the power of words. The same applies to the tone in which you deliver them. How effective would your verbal commands be toward an adversary if you gave those commands as though you were reading a bedtime story? Likewise, how effective is a conversation going to be with your spouse if you deliver your words in the same way you issue verbal commands in a hot situation on duty? There is power in the tone of your voice to either bless or devastate your marriage.

You know the power of command, but when communicating with your spouse, it's important to make your spouse feel like a priority in every way. This will not come easily, my warrior brothers and sisters, and will require intentional daily effort. Remember that friends talk to each other with respect and admiration, and before you were ever spouses or lovers, you were friends. Today, think about how your tone could dilute or tarnish conversation with your spouse and how your tone could add flavor and taste. It's the little things that add up over time, and failing to communicate effectively in your marriage leads to trouble down the road.

Quick Tip

Before you respond to your spouse today, take a second and consider the tone you are conveying. It is often impossible to convey the intended tone through text messages. Commit to spending more time communicating face-to-face instead of via text. In fact, save the "hard stuff" for in-person communication only. If you want to create room for open and honest conversation, a loving, respectful, and gracious tone will establish trust, encourage love, and invite future discussion. Take a few minutes before responding if you feel tempted to respond in a negative tone. Does your conversation reflect grace, or does it incite strife and contention?

Sheepdog

You may not be in a position to communicate with your spouse during your tour, but if you are, be sure to remember they may not be aware of the stressors you are facing at the moment. Strive to use a conversational tone that reflects love and invites future discussion. Your tone, not just your words, can cause deep-rooted emotional pain for your spouse. Consider using tactical breathing techniques before engaging with your spouse or asking for a few minutes after you return home from duty to decompress. Your spouse may request the same from you! Today, think about how your spouse may perceive your tone, not just the words you speak. A word whispered in love is better received than one delivered harshly.

Spouse

Discuss conversational tone with your spouse. Your tone of voice can bring your warrior peace and help them relax at home. There is no "off" switch for your sheepdog, but having a haven to come home to can create a place for them to relax. Both of you have your own stressors and triggers, but remembering you are on the same team, fighting for one purpose and governed by the same loving God, can be a powerful tool in taming the tone of conversation.

Questions for Discussion

- What do you think your tone of conversation is?
- What does your tone convey to your spouse? Ask him or her.

Heavenly Father, help us remember that all we say to each other in our marriage, and the way we say it, conveys either the love you have shown us or contention and strife. Help us be more intentional with the words we speak to each other and the tone in which we deliver them. May we honor your great name with the way we converse in our marriage today. Amen.

Day 3

The Power of Communication

My dear brothers and sisters, take note of this:
Everyone should be quick to listen,
slow to speak and slow to become angry.

JAMES 1:19

Spending time together was something Sean and Kim used to enjoy, but the past eighteen months had taken a toll on their communication. Sean had spent three deployments in the Middle East, and Kim was concerned with his recent change in behavior. It seemed as if the slightest thing would set him off into an angry outburst.

"Sean, please stop yelling at me. All I wanted to know was if you would pick up the kids from school this afternoon. I've been called in to work early and cannot get away in time."

"I told you I am busy, please stop nagging me!" he yelled.

"What is the deal, Sean? Is something going on? We can't accomplish anything if we can't talk to each other." Kim was pleading for her husband to communicate. "I'm not one of your subjects, you know? I am your wife. You don't have to talk to me like I am one of your subjects or a criminal."

Aggressive communication in marriage is a good way to escalate a situation instead of bringing peace into the home. When communicating about work-related issues, set boundaries and stick within those boundaries. If you need to talk about something work-related with someone other than your spouse, then by all means do so. Along with this, you can arrange with your spouse to spend the first ten to fifteen minutes at home enjoying family without any questions about work. Others find it beneficial to use their first moments at home to decompress in silence. Tell your spouse "I love you" before departing for duty or ending a call, as this can be a powerful reminder for both of you when you are apart.

Communication is a two-way street, and there are many factors to ensure the success of your marriage as it relates to communicating with your spouse. After you've been on duty for many hours, it may seem natural to carry the authoritative tone you use on the job over into your home life, but this is seldom a useful approach.

Quick Tip

Communication is both verbal and non-verbal (eye contact, body language, or physical touch). Today, focus on verbal communication, and in particular, the tone of your voice. Don't allow your emotions to take over the conversation, raise your voice, or talk over each other. A simple courtesy is to wait until your spouse finishes talking and then speak. If you are within close range, raising your voice is unnecessary and a communication killer. You can say the right things, but if they are not spoken with the proper tone of voice, the message will not be clearly received. Speak with love and grace when talking with your spouse.

Sheepdog

There may be times when certain triggers (the things that set you off) in a conversation cause your blood pressure to rise. Don't let those things control you. Make sure your spouse is aware of these triggers, and strive to communicate with kindness and gentle humility even if your spouse yells or uses a negative tone.

Spouse

The tone of conversation with your spouse can shift at any moment based on emotions or other external and internal factors. The previous day's events, past trauma and/or drama, or unmet expectations can all play a role in the tone of a conversation. If you or your spouse speak with harshness or sarcastic tones during serious discussions, try to discover the underlying reason for the behavior.

Questions for Discussion

- What are your conversational triggers? Calmly and considerately share them.
- What can you do to help each other overcome the triggers that affect you?

Heavenly Father, we thank you for our marriage and for each other. Please help us be clear, quick listeners, slow to anger, slow to respond, and effective in our communication with each other. Show us the power of communication and the deep level of intimacy awaiting us. Amen.

Resiliency in Marriage

> Though one may be overpowered, two can defend themselves. A cord of three strands is not quickly broken.
>
> ECCLESIASTES 4:12

While the numbers and research vary, there is no doubt divorce is a major issue in America—especially in those marriages where one or both spouses are first responders or members of the military. For some, the long hours and lack of parenting support can present serious problems. For others, unhealthy coping mechanisms (like substance abuse or unfaithfulness) and the inability or refusal to communicate with each other take their toll. Whatever the reason, the devastation caused by divorce in families across America is clear as it becomes an acceptable societal norm.

So how can you prepare yourself and fortify your marriage, building a strong relationship that's resilient in the face of adversity? As with anything in the life of a sheepdog, it begins and ends with your mind-set.

You are each other's partner, the ultimate backup officer, and there shouldn't be anything else you depend on more than your spouse. I said it. You shouldn't depend on anyone or anything else more than your spouse, but that also means you should be delivering more to your spouse in order to meet their needs. It is time to protect your home and your marriage so that when you reach your eternal reward, you'll hear, "Well done!"

Quick Tip

The definition of the word *resiliency*, according to the Merriam-Webster Dictionary, is "an ability to recover from or adjust to misfortune or change."[1] Don't be so rigid in your expectations of each other that you have no room to adjust in the moment of adversity. Offer grace to your spouse and work together to establish a resilient marriage! Build your marriage on a foundation that permits you both to rebound from adversity and remember why you started your journey together. The driving motive behind any two people willing to work through adversity in a relationship is love. How tough is your love? Today, consider ways you can strengthen the pillars of your marriage: love, trust, communication, forgiveness, and intimacy.

Sheepdog

One of the key focuses of your communication efforts should be to promote cohesiveness in your relationship. "A cord of three strands is not quickly broken," but if those strands do not bond, they will not stay together. You can do your part to not only invite future conversation in your marriage but also promote unity, cohesiveness, and effective bonding. One way you can do this is to contribute to your relationship with a sincere, genuine, and heartfelt desire to communicate regularly, as this also causes you to improve the togetherness that is so vital to a bulletproof marriage.

1   *Merriam-Webster.com*, s.v., "resiliency," https:// www.merriam-webster. com/dictionary/deference.

Spouse

It is a scientific fact that faith plays a crucial role in the resiliency of a sheepdog, but it also plays a critical role in a resilient marriage. Without faith, you feel hopeless, without a future, vision, or purpose. Don't live governed by the tide of your emotions or circumstances, but instead live governed by your desire to communicate with your spouse from a heart that seeks to please and honor God. You can have a tremendous impact on encouraging your spouse's faith journey—a key ingredient in building cohesiveness in your marriage.

Questions for Discussion

- What does a resilient marriage look like to you?
- What is one way today that you can nurture, encourage, and foster faith and cohesiveness in your marriage?

Heavenly Father, we know you have come so that we would have life to the fullest, living in complete victory. We also know this applies to our marriage. Today, we ask you to direct us as we seek to build a resilient marriage around your Word and spending time with you in prayer. Amen.

Confront Communication Monsters

There is no fear in love. But perfect love drives out fear, because fear has to do with punishment. The one who fears is not made perfect in love.

1 JOHN 4:18

Modern technology presents a new world of threats to your relationship if you are not prepared, educated, transparent, and communicating with your spouse. Combined with the long hours away from home and many opportunities for temptation, it doesn't take much for the enemy to drown out God's voice in your life. This ungodly voice creeps in and breeds doubt, fear, and anxiety. Before long, you may find yourself dealing with fear-based issues, not reality. Whether you've experienced broken trust in your relationship or not, do not take for granted the opportunity to prepare yourself for the enemy's attacks against your family and marriage.

Infidelity doesn't start in the bedroom; it begins when boundaries are crossed, when a spouse's priorities start shifting toward someone else. This can happen in a regular texting conversation, social media chat, lunch meetings, or other inappropriate connections. Infidelity begins when you allow someone other than your spouse to meet the needs in your life. But, infidelity doesn't have to be the end.

Chronic infidelity is often the sign of deeper, more significant issues. While a text or interaction on social media may seem fun, if you do not set boundaries for yourself and are not transparent with your spouse about what is going on, it can lead to a dangerous path of destruction.

Quick Tip

If there are underlying trust issues in your marriage, it's time to hammer out those issues. Why do those issues exist? Past affairs? Assumptions of infidelity? Long hours at work and unmet needs of one or both of you? Take off the gloves, talk with love, and, if needed, seek out a counselor who will walk you through it. Whatever you do, don't quit on your marriage. Set a date with no children, no distractions, and make sure your supervisors know you will be unavailable. Take your spouse and get away. Talk with each other. Have dinner away from town, do things together that stray from your same old routine. Surprise your spouse. Have an honest conversation about passwords, social media, smartphones, and transparency. Be kind with your spouse. Remember—you are both on the same team!

Sheepdog

In an interview with approximately two dozen spouses of first responders and military service members, one of the biggest "asks" from them was for their sheepdog to be an open, transparent communicator. If you want to develop a deep, passionate, lasting intimacy in your marriage, talk to your spouse. Don't just have business discussions all the time about the serious stuff. Enjoy each other. Enjoy spending time with each other.

Spouse

You have tremendous power to bring peace to your spouse's life. Your words, your touch, and your actions can have a profound impact. What a tremendous responsibility you both hold to speak peace, life, love, and vision into your spouse until death separates you. Today, resolve that you will no longer allow communication monsters to dilute, disempower, or divide your gift as a spouse.

Questions for Discussion

- What is one way you can foster an open line of transparent communication with your spouse?
- What is one way to bring peace into your spouse's life?

Heavenly Father, thank you for arming us with the knowledge needed to have a successful, loving, and peaceful marriage. We want you to be at the center of our home, marriage, and lives. We ask you to remove any guilt, shame, or doubts of past trust issues and give us wisdom as we move forward in unity and love. Amen.

The Proper Time for Everything

There is a time for everything,
and a season for every activity under the heavens.

ECCLESIASTES 3:1

Whether it is working a local municipal patrol beat, running a military operation, or battling another emergency, strategy plays a part in all you do. There's a significant amount of planning that goes into any operation for good reason. You never begin your tour with the intention to fail, as victory is the only acceptable outcome. In the same way, be mindful of the timing when you engage in important conversations with your spouse. This isn't a suggestion to be rigid in your approach to talking with each other, but rather, to be mindful and in tune with the events of your spouse's life.

Every marriage has its own unique challenges, but each marriage requires effective and adequate conversation. There's a proper time for everything under the sun, and this applies to the timing of certain conversations with your spouse. You may be tempted to bombard your spouse with grievances as soon as he or she arrives home: parenting issues, financial turmoil, or other pressing matters. However, the conversation may yield a more positive outcome if it is broached at a different time. No matter the topic of discussion, proper timing can mean the difference between a successful resolution or further strife. Make room for the challenges and stress your spouse faces daily, no matter your role in society.

Quick Tip

With unpredictable schedules, it may be difficult to set a specific time to have discussions about difficult topics. But, whenever possible, do so. Maybe the ideal time is before anyone else in the home is awake, or after everyone else has gone to bed. Find a time that is amicable for both of you to engage in the conversation and give your full attention to each other. You know the value of time, and when you apply that respect and appreciation to the time you have with each other, you will see a return on your investment. Commit to communicate in a healthy, loving, effective manner.

Sheepdog

Most of your shift is spent rushing to arrive on the scene of a call or respond to a crisis in the shortest amount of time as safely as possible, so you know the importance of timing. If your spouse is already overwhelmed with stress from issues in life, don't add to their stress and trigger a potential overload. Respect the fact that, while they weren't in the trenches as you were, they may have had a stressful day too dealing with their own unique challenges and issues. Don't make your stresses a higher priority than those of your spouse. Let your spouse know you need to talk and then find a time that works for you both to discuss things.

Spouse

The more time you spend with your spouse, the more intimately you will know him or her. Both of you are valuable, and both of you face unique challenges every day. Having respect for each other and offering grace when mistakes occur is critical. Don't take out your stress hastily on your spouse or children. You know your spouse better than anyone. You know their quirks, habits, and routines—both the good and bad. Find a time that is conducive for conversation and spend time together talking. Talk with your spouse about their thoughts on the timing of conversations.

Questions for Discussion

- When is the best time to bring up important issues for discussion with your spouse?
- If the time isn't right, what can be a kind way to tell your spouse that the timing is not right but also schedule a time for discussion?

Heavenly Father, give us wisdom and discernment to know the proper time to have important discussions or introduce certain topics. Help us show each other grace in times of need and surrender the stressors of life to you alone. Amen.

Strategy Is Paramount

Surely you need guidance to wage war,
and victory is won through many advisers.

PROVERBS 24:6

The battle plan for marital conflict can be found throughout the Bible. Often we err in marriage when we place a higher priority on being "right" or on our desire to "win" in a conflict instead of serving our spouse and honoring God in our marriage. For many men and women, it is not in their DNA to lose. But in fact, in marriage, we lose when we desire to win at all costs—including causing division in our marriage and emotional pain to our spouse. So, what is the right strategy for conversing with your spouse? Surrender the notion that you must be right or win the conversation. Your spouse is precious in the sight of God, and He gave His all to redeem them.

Your strategy in marital conversations should always begin with the knowledge that God's presence leads us to be gracious, kind, and respectful. Words, timing of discussions, and even the tone of conversations play a role in either nurturing or diluting the intimacy between you and your spouse. It is paramount to have a strategy for regular communication with your spouse, but it is also necessary to establish boundaries for righteous fighting. It's not a matter of *if* there will be marital disagreements, but *when*. Prepare now for those times and you will grow closer through the challenges that come. When you and your spouse are equipped with a clear roadmap for communication, you reduce the potential for the small disagreements to become major issues.

Quick Tip

In a time when marriages are being attacked from every direction, protect the intimacy in your marriage. This requires strategy, planning, and determination. Be aware, however, that this is not always easy or pretty. It means you are willing to do the dirty work in order to enjoy the beautiful aspects of marriage. Don't underestimate the power of communicating with your spouse about these issues. Conversations are the powertrain of intimacy in your marriage. Just as you plan where your money will go each paycheck, allot time for communication. When you and your spouse talk, communicate clearly and leave nothing open to interpretation.

Sheepdog

What is your ideal outcome from your communication efforts in your marriage? The goal should always include a resolved central issue, peace, and a closer relationship with your spouse. Contribute to that ideal by providing fuel for the conversation. Be gentle, kind, gracious, and forgiving. This is not indicative of weakness, rather it is characteristic of a healthy marriage and a present spouse. Your strategy for today is to enter conversation with your spouse while shrouded with grace, love, mercy, and understanding. It may require extra effort on your part to not seem overbearing or forceful, but that extra effort will produce tremendous results.

Spouse

All first responders have odd schedules and few are ever completely off duty. As someone married to a first responder, you know firsthand the challenges this presents and the disruption it can cause in your marriage and family life. One thing you can do is ask your spouse to give you some options for times to talk. Create an inviting environment conducive to open and loving discussion. This can be something as simple as asking your spouse for a time to sit and talk, but don't leave the impression something is wrong! Leaving expectations unspoken and unmet is dangerous and creates room for division in your home.

Questions for Discussion

- What do you feel is the goal of communication in your marriage?
- What are some unspoken expectations that you have?

Heavenly Father, we are thankful for each other and for our marriage. We are thankful to you for the challenges we have faced, but now we seek to have a clear direction for communicating with each other and you. Let us always remember the words we speak echo through all eternity, and what we sow in discord will manifest division. Help us honor you in our communication. Amen.

Tearing Down the Wall

Do nothing out of selfish ambition or vain conceit.
Rather, in humility value others above yourselves.

PHILIPPIANS 2:3

There are different philosophies on how to address communication issues in marriage. An important step is to identify and unlearn some negative habits developed over time. When it comes to negative habits and communication in marriage, one of the deadliest is shutting down. It may seem innocent at the time and may even seem like the best option to overcome the conflict at the moment, but shutting down leads to withdrawal and other unhealthy emotional behaviors. Shutting down during a conversation with your spouse is typically triggered by the desire to avoid conflict, reduce the stress of confrontation, and feel less overwhelmed. While it may solve the short-term conflict, the issue at hand remains unaddressed and will emerge again.

One way to address shutting down or stonewalling in marriage is to have a conversation with your spouse outside of conflict. God's Word promises He will give us peace and comfort, but nowhere are we instructed to comfort ourselves with our own efforts. We are also instructed to respect, love, and submit to each other. None of these characteristics from God's Word involve ignoring our spouse or avoiding confrontation. The best way to navigate through this issue is to address it from a loving perspective. Maybe your negative habits don't include shutting down or stonewalling, and you raise your voice instead or use insulting language toward your spouse. Today is a new day. While it may not always be feasible to pray together before a conversation, you can pray together daily. When you do this, you will find your conversations become healthier, more loving, and more productive.

Quick Tip

Tearing down the walls in marital communication requires diligent and consistent work, but it also requires prayer. Everything revolves around a solid relationship with Christ and having a Christ-focused marriage. If past negative circumstances are causing issues such as stonewalling, the power of prayer, godly counsel, and consistently working together can bring healing and resolution. Recognize the signs of shutting down in yourself—increased heart rate, a lump in your throat, racing thoughts, sweaty palms—take some deep breaths, and share with your spouse how you are feeling. Ask them to help you walk through it together.

Sheepdog

If you notice that you begin to shut down in a conversation with your spouse, think about this: You are leaving a door open for the enemy to infiltrate your marriage. Work to eliminate the threat now. If you see signs such as crossed arms, slouched shoulders, or withdrawal from conversation that indicate your spouse is beginning to shut down, ask open-ended questions to soften the atmosphere. There are times when it is best to give the issue a break and allow both of you to cool off and then return to engage the topic again. Lay it on the table today. If you have been shutting down and ignoring your spouse during communication conflicts, talk to them about your struggles. Instead of shutting down and ignoring the issue, think about why you don't want to address it. Is it fatigue? Fear? Talk to your spouse today about the reasons either of you shut down during conversation and seek a resolution together.

Spouse

Your sheepdog may shut down depending on recent events or overall stress. You must also consider recent traumatic events your spouse may not reveal to you. A gentle approach with proper timing, bathed in love, will probably lead to an open discussion. When you are both willing, discuss the signs of shutting down, why you do it, and how you can both work together to overcome it.

Questions for Discussion

- What causes you to shut down in communication?
- What helps you to not shut down?

Heavenly Father, thank you for the gift of communication and the beauty of marriage. We ask for you to help us better communicate with each other in ways we can both grasp and understand. May every word we speak honor you today. Amen.

Respect the Relationship

For we are God's handiwork, created in Christ Jesus to do good works, which God prepared in advance for us to do.

EPHESIANS 2:10

"When you step up to the line, do not remove your weapon from the holster until instructed to do so," the range master shouted one muggy afternoon. "Remember muzzle discipline. Eyes and ears, folks! Range is hot!"

Most of you know the ensuing sound of firearms sending ammo down range followed by the "clink-clank" of brass hitting the ground nearby. You were, from day one, taught weapon safety and respect for your weapon. You weren't taught to fear a firearm, but rather, to respect its design, power, and use. Likewise, respecting your relationship with your spouse is necessary for optimum satisfaction in marriage.

When things get tough—and things *will* get tough at some point—you need to remember why you married your spouse. Remember why you started dating, what attracted you to them, and the lifelong goals you shared in the beginning. You will face challenges in your marriage as a first responder or military service member, but respect the relationship you have with your spouse. Just as you would be mindful and professional with your service weapon or other tools on duty, remember that communication in marriage is an essential tool that requires skill and desire to be useful. Your communication skills with your spouse can grow rusty, and it is necessary to practice these skills daily. Both you and your spouse are God's handiwork, created in Christ Jesus for His purpose. Before you fire off words you cannot take back, remember to respect the relationship and tame your tongue.

Quick Tip

Respecting your work equipment means you maintain it, use it, and are not careless with it. Approach your marriage with the same respect. Don't talk negatively about your spouse to others, and don't address conflict publicly. Demonstrating honor and respect will help you both have a long, fruitful marriage together. Just one small word or action a day to improve your marriage can go a long way, and then, after one year, you will have taken 365 steps toward a bulletproof marriage. Leave each other hidden love notes today and provide hints to help your spouse find them.

Sheepdog

Think of all the things and people in life you respect, and you will find that you are more likely to show care toward those people, relationships, things, or situations. Too often we are tempted to just live on autopilot instead of demonstrating that we care about our marriage. Don't fall victim to apathy because things have been tough in the past. Take a new perspective on the way you view your marriage. Put forth a fresh effort, show you care, and watch God do the rest. Your actions of obedience to the instructions found in God's Word will lead to new life.

Spouse

Marriage can be a beautiful blessing as God intended, or it can be a burden that shortens your life. The fact is, too often we seek to have a good marriage without having Christ at the center of it all. Think about how much more peaceful your life would be if He was the center of every issue and if you measured every success according to His standard in the Word of God.

Questions for Discussion

- What is one way you can show care in your relationship today that is meaningful for your spouse?
- What is one way you can demonstrate respect for your marriage today that is meaningful for your spouse?

Heavenly Father, thank you for giving me the spouse of my dreams. I ask you to help me see my spouse as a gift from you and to see them as you see them. Help us communicate clearly as two people created for your handiwork. Amen.

Don't Let This Pass You By

But you desire honesty from the womb,
teaching me wisdom even there.

PSALM 51:6 NLT

Ignoring a wound will not help it heal. Finding the path of least resistance in your marital communications will lead to more severe consequences and leave room for the enemy to infiltrate your marriage. The foundation of your marriage requires honesty and transparency, and that means working to overcome negative conversation habits. One of those negative habits is adopting a passive-aggressive attitude. Don't sweep a major issue under the rug. Instead, deal with the issue in a respectable, loving, and honorable manner. A spouse who is passive-aggressive may sulk, pout, or use other means to avoid direct confrontation. This is not healthy for your marriage and should be addressed.

You may think, *What does that have to do with honesty?* Passive-aggressive behavior in marital communication is dishonest because it is not revealing the whole truth of who you are, what you think, and what you desire to communicate. If this is a problem for you, first think about why you want to avoid confrontation with your spouse on an issue. Maybe a past incident is causing you to believe this confrontation will turn sour. Today is a new day. Begin the discussion with prayer and ask God to help you create an inviting and open atmosphere for honest dialogue. He can provide you both with the wisdom and grace to navigate through your negative communication habits. Don't let this moment pass you by! It's a turning point for your marriage—a milestone.

Quick Tip

The keys to identifying negative communication habits are prayer, transparency, and vulnerability. Don't dodge the hard stuff in your marriage. Ignoring a wound doesn't cause it to stop bleeding or heal itself if medical attention is required. Your marriage requires the same attention and effort. Your spouse is worth the effort just as much now as they were when you were dating. Root out those negative things and replace them with healthy, holy, and open discussion.

Sheepdog

From conception, God has called you to live a life of integrity, to follow His plan for you, and to honor Him in all you do, even in your marriage discussions. Addressing these negative communication patterns in marriage will not be easy, but it is necessary to grow. Think of it as pruning the branches. Prune the vines to get the most beneficial and healthy harvest from your marriage. Write down one thing you can do to improve communication between you and your spouse, share it with your spouse, and then pray about it together.

Spouse

Your marriage matters, and you matter to God. Life won't always be easy, but committing to face the tough things in marriage and life together means you do it every single time as a team. It's easy to ignore the core issues in marriage, but this will not lead to growth or healing. Doing one small thing together every day to improve your marriage means you're working toward a more perfect marriage, even if it doesn't seem so perfect today. Write down one thing you can do to improve communication between you and your spouse, share it with your spouse, and then pray about it together.

Questions for Discussion

- How can you build in more time to talk with your spouse? What can be pruned to create more time?
- What negative communication habits have developed over time, and what is one good habit you want to build?

Heavenly Father, open our eyes to see the negative communication habits we have developed in our marriage. We seek to honor you in this union and ask for your discernment, wisdom, and guidance in eliminating the bad habits and creating healthy, holy, and lasting habits to honor you with in our marriage. Amen.

You're Not a Robot

As a face is reflected in water,
so the heart reflects the real person.

PROVERBS 27:19 NLT

A constant tug-of-war between two people in marriage is exhausting, and it destroys a couple's intimacy. When you refuse to compromise and negotiate within the boundaries of your relationship, you send a message to your spouse that you are selfish and their needs and viewpoint are not important. There are non-negotiables, but overall, healthy compromise and negotiation are two areas to diligently work on. In order to reflect the heart of God in your marriages, you must put your spouse before yourself. That's the truest demonstration of love. Your actions and willingness to serve your spouse will reflect your true heart.

When you and your spouse are having a difficult time agreeing on an issue, think about it from this perspective: Is your position of being "right" worth the peace in your home? Take care to avoid using this call to compromise and negotiate as an excuse to become passive when things are challenging—that's not the objective at all. Be flexible and adaptable, willing to give and not just take. Place your spouse's views and desires before your own. One of the most critical components of marriage is learning that communication, compromise, and negotiation are all very much like a graceful dance. A successful dance requires two people who are willing to give each other a generous margin of error.

Quick Tip

It is necessary to determine boundaries in your relationships because they establish an equitable playing field for communicating, negotiating, and compromise. They exist to give you freedom and keep you from undue harm. Some boundaries will be issues you disagree on, such as finances, parenting, in-laws, holiday traditions, or career decisions. There's nothing wrong with being passionate about your stance, but love your spouse in all you do. Have an open discussion with your spouse today about three issues that, to you, are non-negotiable. Identify where there is no room for compromise and then listen as your spouse shares their non-negotiables with you.

Sheepdog

My fellow warrior, there is a time to use your sword in battle, but your spouse is not your enemy. Lay down your sword and conduct your interactions with your spouse with a soft hand, a loving touch, and a gentle word. This does not mean you are a weakling, and it does not reveal a soft, open spot in your armor as a warrior sheepdog. It is quite the opposite. It reveals tremendous strength and power, reaffirming your call to serve not only your community but also your spouse with excellence and love. The doors for negotiation and compromise in marriage are often opened with a gentle touch, not a forceful blow.

Spouse

As you grasp the hands of your sheepdog, grant him or her margin for error. They live and operate in a zero-defect profession. In their world of work, there are no allowances for mistakes on duty, and that mind-set often carries over into the home. Communicating the things that are not open for compromise and negotiation allows more leeway in areas that are open for such things. Establish boundaries through open, honest, and loving communication. Let your spouse know you will negotiate on certain issues.

Questions for Discussion

- What area in your marriage needs negotiation? Why?
- How can each of you move toward the other's preference on this issue so you can find middle ground?

Heavenly Father, we thank you for giving us clear, biblically based boundaries for our marriage. We know these exist for our own well-being. May our conversation with each other be clothed with grace today and every day, and may we have a heart that fights to give more to our spouse than defend what we perceive is rightfully ours. Amen.

Close the Gap

You can recognize fools by the way they give full vent to their rage and let their words fly! But the wise bite their tongue and hold back all they could say.

PROVERBS 29:11 TPT

When was the last time you were reading an article online or the comments on a social media post and saw how rude, vile, and unrestrained some folks can be? It's easy to allow your emotions to control what you say through text messages or email because there are no immediate perceived repercussions. However, words—whether typed or spoken—can cause irreparable harm to the recipient. Especially in moments of correction or disagreement, words should be spoken in person and with love. There is no challenge in letting venomous words fly; the challenge is bridling your tongue—especially when emotions are on the line. God has given you a much higher and better way to address these issues, not only in your marriage but also in all your communications.

Knowing the deepest pain often comes from those you love the most should drive you to guard your tongue and protect your spouse. There are several things the enemy uses to create distance and division between you and your spouse. Having a heated discussion via text is one of those strategies. It is difficult to accurately determine emotional tone through a text, but it is easy to deliver words lacking love and grace. Marriage thrives on intimacy, and relying too heavily on digital communication with your spouse is one way to destroy that intimacy. Suggest to your spouse that your relationship with him or her is more valuable than an exchange of text messages and you would rather have the conversation in person.

Quick Tip

"Closing the gap" in your marriage means removing the things that divide you and your spouse. Don't allow other people, their opinions, their suggestions, or anything else to come between the two of you. Even the wisest person knows the fruits of their rage and anger are negative emotions. These emotions can also create a gap of division and contention in your marriage. Ensure nothing divides your marriage. Protect it. It is for you, together with your spouse, to do the work to nurture, protect, and grow your relationship. Today, identify gap-makers and divisive issues or people and place some distance between your marriage and them.

Sheepdog

While exchanging text messages and phone calls are primary methods of communicating in the twenty-first century, handwritten notes have never lost their effect. Consider writing a few words on paper and leave it in a place your spouse can find it later. Don't give in to the temptation to express your rage and anger through text messages or in person. Control those negative emotions. It is easy to protect marriage from outside threats, but it is just as easy to create division with a negative attitude and hurtful words. Resolve to speak with love, protect your marriage, and talk openly with grace.

Spouse

For your spouse, who often faces life and death situations on duty, "closing the gap" means it's time to engage the enemy. Sometimes this occurs immediately, at other times it occurs after the situation has been assessed in more detail. The key here is that at some point closing the gap, engaging the subject, and resolving the issue is required. This takes courage and skill. These same theories apply in your marriage. There are just some things you cannot address from a distance or through a phone.

Questions for Discussion

- What is dividing you as a couple?
- What is one way you can close the gap and protect your marriage today?

Heavenly Father, thank you for giving us the blessing of marriage. Help us respect our relationship with each other and honor you by communicating more in person than we do on the phone or by text messages. Never let us lose sight of the joy of having each other in this life. Amen.

The Art of Mutual Submission

And further, submit to one another
out of reverence for Christ.

EPHESIANS 5:21 NLT

Friends have a unique way of treating each other. Think about
going out to a restaurant for a meal with a friend, or maybe you've
met someone at a restaurant, and then the bill arrives. Have you
ever witnessed someone fight over who was going to pay the bill? It
seems crazy to do something like that, but it demonstrates respect
and generosity to the other person. Sometimes it is necessary to
give without any further expectation, and other times it is necessary
to receive with open hands. When you choose to favor your spouse
over yourself, you are saying to them, "You are more important
than me having my own way. You matter more to me than anything
right now, and I want to place you on a pedestal above others in
this world."

When two married people choose to willfully submit to one
another and favor the needs of their spouse over their own, it is a
physical demonstration of the love of God. He favored our own
eternal life, our salvation, our victory in this life over His own life.
If total selflessness is the key to finding deep joy in your marriage,

then selfishness is the root of most marital conflict. It is written in God's Word that men should love their wives as Christ loved the church, and we can all agree Christ was not selfish in the way He loved us when He walked this earth, and He is not selfish with His love now. Practicing mutual submission and favoring your spouse over your own desires may be tough at first, but as you drift further away from your old way of thinking, you will find tremendous freedom and joy in your marriage.

Quick Tip

A selfish person will ruin the most fruitful blessings in life. A person who demands respect from another does not understand the nature of God, nor do they understand the concept of respect. You cannot demand that your spouse submit to you, but you can cultivate a relationship that invites mutual submission when you submit first and often. Lay down pride, repent of selfishness, abandon the need to be right, and serve your spouse. Be willing to lose a fight with your spouse. After all, you are in this together, on the same team, fighting for the same goal. Do what is best for your spouse and your marriage—respect and submission will follow.

Sheepdog

The personality type of many first responders and military personnel is an aggressive, type A, "Alpha" personality. This means that at times the sheepdog can seem overbearing or even authoritarian. While your heart may be in the right place, you have to communicate in a way that can be heard and received by your spouse. Be excellent at your job on the streets or on duty, but at home, be gentle, kind, compassionate, and loving. Mutual submission doesn't mean you are a doormat or no longer have a say in decision-making; it means you prefer your spouse's happiness over your own.

Spouse

Your spouse will likely never lose their warrior-protector spirit. It's in their nature. Mutual submission is an art which requires effort, commitment, and dedication to the mission. Ask your spouse how he or she defines submission in marriage. Offer your definition. Then together examine what the Bible says about submission in marriage.

Questions for Discussion

- What do you feel mutual submission should look like in your marriage?
- What is one way you can demonstrate a heart of humility, submission, and servant-leadership to your spouse today?

Heavenly Father, thank you for the example of submission throughout your Word. Thank you for sending your own son to die for us so we could have eternal life. We ask you to give us the strength and heart to prefer our spouse over our own desires and passionately rekindle the spark in our marriage. Amen.

Keep Your Word

Don't make rash promises, and don't be hasty in bringing matters before God. After all, God is in heaven, and you are here on earth. So let your words be few.

ECCLESIASTES 5:2 NLT

Miscommunication in marriage is a silent killer of intimacy. It's creating an ever-growing wedge between you and your spouse, creating conflict where it doesn't belong. Sometimes you are both so busy trying to make ends meet that you don't have time to slow down and focus on each other. To avoid miscommunication while talking to your spouse, devote your full attention to him or her. Think about it this way: Would you give your life for your spouse? Then give your best to them when they are talking and demonstrate the fact that you value them. Keeping your promises is one key way to show your spouse how much they mean to you.

It's not only the big things that can cause strife, like not holding up your end of the deal. Rather, it is often a collection of little issues—taking out the trash, changing the air filter, paying a bill, or running an errand. Neglecting the simple things can cause undue frustration. When you make an effort to keep your promises and clearly communicate with your spouse, you are showing them how much you value, honor, and respect them as a person and as your lover. Neglecting the small things leads to major issues, even when the promises seem insignificant. Failing to keep those promises can convey a message that you do not value your spouse highly.

Quick Tip

Think about your reaction to finding out someone has lied to you, or how you'd feel about being on the receiving end of a broken promise. If your spouse tells you they will do something, you expect them to do it. Promises establish a given expectation between two parties that should lead to a positive outcome. Today, be intentional about keeping your word with your spouse, no matter how insignificant it may seem.

Sheepdog

This may seem extraordinarily fundamental and simple, but keeping your word to your spouse is the very foundation of your marriage. You exchanged vows on your wedding day, just as you promised to uphold the Constitution as part of your professional oath. Keeping your word is in your nature—it's who you are. If you have a reputation of not doing what you tell your spouse you will do, you are communicating to your spouse that they are not valuable to you—they are not worth your commitment. In all things, remember to let your spouse know their value in your life.

Spouse

If your spouse has failed to keep a promise in the past, know they are working to improve on that track record starting today. Effort is invaluable. When two people are willing to hold each other accountable and keep the promises they've made, they can have a lifelong friendship and a thriving marriage.

Questions for Discussion

- What is one way you can fulfill a promise to your spouse today, no matter how simple?
- What is one way today that you can foster an atmosphere in your marriage that encourages kept promises?

Heavenly Father, thank you that your promises are always "yes" and "amen." Help us keep our word to each other in our marriage, no matter how insignificant it may seem. Remind us of the power of fulfilled vows and the benefits and blessings of keeping our word to each other. Amen.

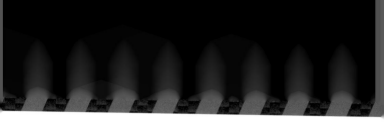

Talk about Parenting

Experiencing many corrections and rebukes
will make you wise. But if left to your own ways,
you'll bring disgrace to your parents.

PROVERBS 29:15 TPT

Many spouses come from broken homes—homes where their
parents were divorced or where some form of abuse was present.
Nobody wants to talk about these things, but it is necessary to
find healing and build a strong marriage. Even if you both come
from parents who never divorced and had outstanding marriages,
you come from different lives. You bring your own ideas about
parenting, discipline, and the education of your children. It is
very possible that you have special memories of holiday traditions
as a child, but those may not be shared by your spouse. If this
is left uncommunicated, it can lead to unmet expectations and
unnecessary conflict. Whether you have children now or plan to
have children in the future, talking about these expectations is
critical to your success both as a married couple and as parents.

With so many books, courses, classes, and theories on
parenting, it can be easy to become overwhelmed and confused
about the direction you should follow with your own children.

Demonstrating love and affection for your spouse in front of your children can be a healthy method for showing the love of God to them. In contrast, yelling, name-calling, or abusive language can scar your children for life. Set a date for just the two of you and use the time to lay out your ideas for parenting if you are currently rearing or plan to raise children together. It sounds so simple, so elementary, but taking time to talk through and establish expectations together will bring you closer and help you develop a stronger bond as parents.

Quick Tip

The main goal here is to make sure you are both on the same team, both invested and interested, and both present as parents. Be prepared to adapt to new ideas your spouse may have about parenting that you're not familiar with. Don't be afraid to fail, but if you fail, fail together. Having an unshakeable bond as a couple, knowing you will be raising your children as one body, will create a healthy home life for your entire family.

Sheepdog

Not everyone who is married has children. But, if you do, be present when you are home. Be interested in the activities and interests of your child. Don't spend more time with hobbies than you do being a parent. Your child needs you to show them the way with a loving, caring hand, not an authoritarian, impersonal presence. Nobody can impart into your child what you have, and you only get one shot to do it right.

Spouse

There are many ideas around the issue of parenting, but ultimately the best one is the one that works for your family. Resist the temptation to be overly critical of your spouse's approach as a parent. If there is an issue you disagree on, do not address it in front of your children. Always present a united front. Take time to discuss together how best to support each other.

Questions for Discussion

- What is one thing you can do today to be more present as a parent?
- What is one thing you can do to support your spouse as you parent together?

Heavenly Father, thank you for the gift of investing in the life of a child. Give us the wisdom to see that our lives on this earth are temporary and that the best thing we can do as one united body is to invest in the lives of children. Amen.

Treasure for Two

"No one can serve two masters. Either you will hate the one and love the other, or you will be devoted to the one and despise the other. You cannot serve both God and money."

MATTHEW 6:24

If you had all the money you needed to live a comfortable life, with plenty of margin between your income and expenses, do you think you would still have disagreements or conflict with your spouse regarding finances? If you and your spouse have different ideas, plans, or even different budgets, you will find discussing finances to be a volatile issue that creates much strife in your marriage. Being in agreement on money is not as easy as it sounds, especially if you don't have enough of it to meet your basic needs. It doesn't matter if you have a lot or a little; get on the same page about your finances. This is an issue that can quickly get out of control and evolve into a mammoth monster to address.

Once a week, have a conversation about upcoming income, expenditures, and any extra needs in order to keep track of your finances. But don't stop there! Discuss future needs, big-ticket purchases, and dream a little! Talk about a vacation spot you both want to visit and begin saving for it together. On occasion, there is a need for separate budgets, finances, or bank accounts, but in most cases this is not necessary. Financial separation takes away from the unity of the marriage and creates opportunity for division and conflict. At the end of the day, you didn't marry each other because you were eager to be miserable. You loved your spouse. Don't allow finances to dilute or poison that passion.

Quick Tip

Where is your treasure? Is it money and possessions? Are you greedy and materialistic? Those things will all lose their appeal in time and eventually pass away. Chasing fulfillment through material gain is guaranteed to end with emptiness and disappointment. One treasure that never fades is treasure in heaven, and one way to store up that treasure is to treat your spouse like God would have you do. Schedule five minutes today to talk about your finances with your spouse.

Sheepdog

Having one plan, one goal, and one vision for your marriage means you both are paddling the boat in the same direction for the same reason. Sometimes one of you may have to give more effort than usual, and in the case of finances, it may require extreme effort and resiliency to get it done. Challenges will come, whether in the form of tight finances, parenting headaches, health concerns, or other areas, but resolving now to work through those situations together and allowing circumstances to push you closer to each other will position you for victory long before the challenges come.

Spouse

Every couple has their own arrangements, routines, and habits when it comes to finances. Some sit down weekly and discuss financial matters while others seldom, if ever, discuss the issue. If you want a bulletproof marriage, nothing can be off-limits to both of you being involved. Communication fuels unity, and unity births longevity. Commit to serving your spouse in marriage by keeping them informed of financial issues and working together as one.

Questions for Discussion

- What are some expenses coming up that you want to be ready for?
- What is a dream you both have, and how can you begin to save for it?

Heavenly Father, thank you for the continuous provision you give as we honor you with our hearts, lives, and resources. Give us your wisdom as it relates to our financial resources. We ask you today for a heart of giving, to be generous, and to find joy in contentment. Amen.

SECTION TWO

Pillars of Trust

Building Blocks

Her husband can trust her, and she will greatly enrich his life.

PROVERBS 31:11 NLT

"Babe, are you okay?"

John still had moments of terror related to a previous call. Certain triggers would bring back the memory of that call like it had just happened moments ago. His wife, Amy, who had supported him for over fifteen years as he served in law enforcement, had noticed he had gotten quiet and was staring into empty space. John would open up to only a few people in his life, and Amy was one of them. She knew when he needed her most, when he needed a safe place to rest, and he knew he could depend on her in his most difficult moments. This trust was built over many years by taking time to establish a line of communication and having an understanding and respect for the challenges John faced on duty.

While you serve your community, you need to know your spouse has your back—that they are supporting you, praying for you, and waiting for your return home. You can trust your spouse, and they will greatly enrich your life! The fruit of trust

61

and vulnerability in marriage is a passionate, lasting intimacy that cannot be dissuaded by the trivial challenges of life. You know without a doubt that your spouse is on your team and you can trust your life in his or her hands.

Quick Tip

At some point you will need arms to fall into. You will need someone to catch you, to help you, to confide in, to share your darkest secrets with. This is the role of a spouse. Be willing to trust your spouse, falling into their arms, knowing you are completely safe and protected. Though difficulties will arise, you both know the process. You know how to find victory in tribulation. You know as you surrender everything to Him, He will guide you. Do you trust each other 100 percent? Have you demonstrated that trust? Have you maintained that trust? Keep it protected at all costs, and do not compromise it.

Sheepdog

There's nothing wrong with being comfortable with your spouse. It's a natural response to having total trust in your marriage. In fact, one Hebrew word for "trust" in the Old Testament is *careless*. This means you have no need to put on a mask with your spouse. You can be you—relaxed and comfortable. It means you should fall recklessly into the arms of your spouse and love without restraint. Throw off the temptation to keep certain areas of your heart and life off-limits to your spouse—be open and transparent. Your openness and transparency will create an environment for trust to grow.

Spouse

Building trust isn't like the physical construction of a wall or building, where a definitive completion point is evident to all. Think about it like building muscle in your body—the muscle grows over time as it is used and exercised. Building trust is an ongoing process and requires the input and effort of both you and your spouse. When you give 100 percent effort 100 percent of the time for an extended period, you will find that you have the best marriage anyone could dream of. But it takes work. Trust does not come easily, but it can be easily destroyed.

Questions for Discussion

- What does trust look like to you?
- What is one way you can invite deeper trust from your spouse?

Heavenly Father, thank you for showing us both the beauty and necessity to trust you wholeheartedly. We thank you for showing us the benefits of trusting each other and for showing us the boundaries we need to establish in marriage and life. Help us today as we continue to build trust in our marriage. Amen.

Beautiful Restoration

But instead be kind and affectionate toward one another.
Has God graciously forgiven you? Then graciously forgive
one another in the depths of Christ's love.

EPHESIANS 4:32 TPT

Every love story is different, but too often people derive their
perception of romance from what they see in movies or television.
The typical story line follows one person who cautiously trusts
another, falls in love, and then the romantic music plays as they
ride off into life with a loaded bank account before the credits begin
to roll. Seldom does the story line include the scenes when trust
between two lovers is compromised because of a stupid decision
made by one of them. Sometimes, marriage is compromised
because of a lack of self-control. Other times it is the result of
selfishness, but in any case, it damages trust in the process.

Restoring your trust in each other isn't impossible, but
neither is it easy. It does not come overnight. Sometimes you must
start from square one and build from the ground up—creating a
stronger, more resilient marriage in the process. Trust is a fickle
element of any relationship, especially marriages. In a world
where nothing is off-limits and morality is being redefined by the

minority, stay true to who you are, adapt to the issues you face, but more than anything, keep Christ at the center of your marriage. Breaching trust doesn't have as much to do with honesty as it has to do with transparency. If you have relationships outside your marriage that your spouse wouldn't be happy knowing about, that's a breach of trust. It's time to rebuild. It's time to restore. Now is the time to root out any fractured element of trust in your relationship and build a resilient, lasting, life-long marriage.

Quick Tip

Everyone has their own definition of what a breach of trust means. It is helpful to have these things laid out on the table for discussion with each other. Define for yourselves what constitutes a breach of trust in your marriage. For you it may be a single lie or an unkept promise, but the only path to resolving a breach of trust is vulnerability between two people. Be open and honest. To restore trust, you must remove any seed of lies and introduce the power of truth into your relationship. Don't keep secrets outside your marriage—this invites broken trust when the secrets are discovered and brought into the open.

Sheepdog

How boring would life be if the seas were calm all the time? There will come a season in life when calm seas are desired, but warriors crave something to be victorious over, something to conquer. Your marriage requires you to fight for it. Sure, you can sit back and let it drift on autopilot, but don't be jealous of others who have phenomenal marriages—they have put in the work. Today, choose to put in the work, investing in and fighting for your own marriage. Choose to keep it pure and holy, striving for excellence and an atmosphere of trust with your spouse.

Spouse

One of the greatest ways you can support your spouse when they leave for duty is to let them know you trust them, that they can trust you, and you can both work through anything together. Letting them know you are willing to make your marriage not only work but also thrive will empower your spouse and breathe fresh life into your marriage. Sometimes, a genuine effort on the part of both parties is all that is required to create some positive momentum.

Questions for Discussion

- What is one way you can protect the trust between you and your spouse today?
- What is one way you can create the momentum of healing in some unaddressed areas today?

Heavenly Father, we recognize the need for you in our lives, but we also recognize the need for you in our marriage. If we haven't placed you at the center of our relationship before today, we repent and choose to place you front and center. Our marriage cannot thrive without you, without your Word, and without each of us surrendering totally to you. Will you please help mend any areas where trust needs to be restored and where healing is needed? Help our marriage be abundant in all areas. Thank you, Lord. Amen.

Trust the Training

Physical training is good, but training for godliness is much better, promising benefits in this life and in the life to come.

1 TIMOTHY 4:8 NLT

Having complete confidence in your skills is necessary for success in any assignment. The perfect balance between trusting your training and knowing you are prepared for any scenario will help eliminate the worrisome thoughts that may enter the mind of you or your spouse while you are away. The critical element in supporting each other through whatever conflict arises, whether it originates inside the home or externally, is knowing you are both prepared. You know how vital it is to be trained in the unique skills necessary to carry out your professional duties. It is just as vital that you also be prepared physically, emotionally, and spiritually within your marriage.

Find time to spend with Jesus through worship, studying the Bible, and prayer—both individually and together, as this will keep your mission central. These times of praise and discovery together will also serve to balance and steady your marriage, especially when storms come. Think of training for godliness like preparing for duty. You know conflict will come on duty at some point and your supervisors ensure you are up to par on training. When it comes to your marriage, you must make the decision daily to train for any scenario. It's not always easy, but having full confidence and trust in your training and preparation will establish your feet on a firm foundation in your marriage.

Quick Tip

Resolve today for your marriage to become the best marriage it can be according to the metrics of God's Word. Don't fall into the trap of comparing your marriage to other relationships. Your marriage is unique, with its own challenges and dynamics. You cannot compare what God is doing in your life with what He is doing in the lives of others. Today, resolve to work daily on your relationship with each other, committing your lives to Christ and to each other every morning.

Sheepdog

Many of your skills as a first responder or member of the armed services require annual certification training. This is so you will remain proficient in the use of your skills and the tools involved with your trade. The length of most basic training programs is around ninety days for the basic level. What would happen if you entered into an agreement with your spouse for the next ninety days, committing to give your best effort to improve, sharpen, and build your marriage? Today, write out that commitment to your spouse. Dedicate your efforts to improving yourself and your marriage relationship every day in some way, no matter how insignificant it may seem, for the next ninety days.

Spouse

It may be difficult for you to commit to adding anything else to your life right now. But, think about how beautiful your marriage would look, even if it is great right now, by committing to working on it daily for the next ninety days. Training, testing, and preparing—all these things are well-known to your spouse. Join hands, pursue God together through prayer and studying the Bible, and ask God to guide you as you work toward improving not only the trust you have for each other but also your marriage overall.

Questions for Discussion

- What do you think is the top priority God wants you to address in your marriage?
- What is one thing you can commit to today to improve your marriage?

Heavenly Father, thank you for the wisdom to be a great spouse and to pursue holiness, righteousness, and a desire to have an excellent marriage. We refuse to settle for a mediocre marriage, and we refuse to become a statistic. We ask you to guide our steps and bless our pursuit of you as we endeavor to build a bulletproof marriage. Amen.

Affair Proofing

Then Jesus began teaching them with stories: "A man planted a vineyard. He built a wall around it, dug a pit for pressing out the grape juice, and built a lookout tower. Then he leased the vineyard to tenant farmers and moved to another country."

MARK 12:1 NLT

For Zach, it began with a simple text from a coworker asking about how his day was going. The extra attention felt good. It had been a while since Zach's wife, Kim, had shown him any extra attention. Life had gotten busy after the twins were born, and Zach was given a promotion. They didn't even realize they had begun taking each other for granted. Before long, what had been a passionate marriage built on a beautiful friendship had eroded into a home split by unfaithfulness. All it took was a moment of compromise, one moment of submitting to an outside voice who gained prominence inside the marriage. It could have all been avoided by being transparent about the messages, keeping the temptation of outside voices at bay, and prioritizing the marital relationship.

Think of your marriage as a fortress, a castle ruled by the King of Glory, where you and your spouse reside. That castle has boundaries to protect you from the outside influences of the world, providing the necessary protection for you and your spouse. Today it is time to silence those outside voices. It doesn't matter who or what they are. Maybe it's a coworker. Regardless, it doesn't even have to be sexual or intimate in nature to damage your marriage. Those outside voices can not only wreak havoc in your home if you give them the authority to do so, but they can also sow seeds of discord and suspicion, creating a competition in your marriage instead of a flourishing bond.

Quick Tip

The 1974 Bachman–Turner Overdrive hit "Takin' Care of Business" can best describe today's tip to bulletproof your marriage. Take care of your marriage every day, in every way. Don't shy away from the challenges, but don't address the heavy hitters at the wrong moment either. Be kind. Build a fortress around your marriage through prayer, friendship with your spouse, communication, and trust. So many people want to suggest that marriage to one person is outdated and obsolete. Prove them wrong. Take care of business in your marriage by protecting your relationship and loving your spouse well.

Sheepdog

Ultimately it requires both spouses to make a marriage successful, but the power of prayer supersedes everything. No marriage is immune from troublesome times, so take time to prepare yours to endure hardship. Spend quality time with your spouse, initiate meaningful discussion, break up the same-ole-same-ole routines. Take him or her out on a date with no kids and bring the house down! Take those extra moments to treat your spouse like royalty. Make a habit of putting the needs of your spouse before your own.

Spouse

Don't allow suspicious thoughts or worry to creep into your mind and create problems that do not exist. It can affect your mood and cause friction in your marriage. Instead, pray for your marriage and declare God's Word over your home and family. Speak life. Declare victory. The only way to truly affair-proof your marriage is for both of you to remain submitted to Christ and honor each other out of reverence for Him in all you do. Don't allow the enemy to infiltrate your relationship.

Questions for Discussion

- What would be a meaningful way for your spouse to care for you today?
- What would be a meaningful way for your spouse to honor you today?

Heavenly Father, in a world where standards are being demolished daily and anything goes, we ask you to keep our hearts soft and tender and near to you. We ask that you would make us sensitive to respond to the convicting power of the Holy Spirit swiftly. Protect our eyes, ears, and hearts from the temptations and attacks of this world. Place a hedge of protection around our marriage and show us the path to a blessed and thriving relationship. Amen.

Day 21

Addressing Past Hurts

"And when you pray, make sure you forgive the faults of
others so that your Father in heaven will also forgive you.
But if you withhold forgiveness from others, your Father
withholds forgiveness from you."

MATTHEW 6:14–15 TPT

Early in their marriage, Sam's wife confessed to having an affair.
He admitted that the feelings he experienced at that revelation
were confusing and hurtful, and the intimacy in their marriage
was destroyed. Eight years later, Sam and Diane both considered
their marriage to be "good," but it was lacking something. Sam
still resented Diane and even went so far as to say he wasn't sure
he had forgiven her. Diane said she never wanted to talk about
the affair out of shame and guilt. The biggest issues on the table
were unforgiveness, bitterness, and resentment. Neither sought
out professional counseling and tried to navigate the rough waters
alone.

Forgiveness of another's actions neither condones those
actions nor welcomes further negative action. Rather, forgiveness
releases the past hurt and allows God to bring healing and
restoration into the relationship. Past hurt in a marriage can be

difficult to define, but it always involves a breach of intimacy and trust. The only way to address past hurt is to forgive and decide to move forward together. Reconciliation is seldom beyond reach if you both are willing to forgive, pursue healing together, and rebuild trust. Deep inside your heart, determine if there is anything that will separate you from your spouse. There must be established boundaries, and they must be respected. Today, dig up the roots of past hurt and eliminate them once and for all.

Quick Tip

If you want to have a bulletproof marriage, you must be willing to forgive. That's not to say that abuse should ever be tolerated, but it is a requirement of God that we forgive, even if an exit from a relationship is necessary due to abuse. Be quick to forgive, knowing it is up to God and the individual to work out the offenses. Even in the little things, be quick to forgive. Don't allow issues to pile up in your marriage. Talk about them. Eliminate uncommunicated expectations, and seek God for healing and restoration. If you are both free from past hurt, practicing forgiveness remains beneficial to moving forward and protecting your relationship.

Sheepdog

Withholding forgiveness is like having ammo without a firearm. There's absolutely nothing you can do with it. Why would you want to hold on to it? You will, without a doubt, make a mistake in your marriage. Whether it be a minor or major offense, you will need and desire forgiveness from your spouse. Having been the recipient of unending disbursements of God's grace and mercy, you are called upon to give forgiveness freely.

Spouse

Don't suppress your feelings. If you have an issue in your

relationship, address it. Allowing past hurts to fester is like allowing an old wound to heal without any treatment or care. Talk to your spouse. Express how you feel. What if you were both withholding forgiveness and that alone was inhibiting growth in your marriage? Today, take internal stock of your soul. If you are harboring unforgiveness, be willing to lay it down. Even if you want to hold a grudge and stay mad, take a step of faith and give those things to God. Ask Him to help you.

Questions for Discussion

- What grudges does God want you to give to Him?
- What is one way you can release unforgiveness and prevent future pent-up feelings of resentment?

Heavenly Father, we are thankful for your mercy in our marriage, which is new every morning. As two people totally dependent on you, we recognize our faults and ask for your direction and guidance. Help us find healing and restoration from past hurt. Furthermore, we surrender all pain, past hurt, and offenses to you. They are not ours. We lay them down at your feet. Amen.

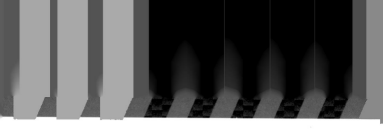

Diluting Trust

Give all your worries and cares to God,
for he cares about you.

1 PETER 5:7 NLT

So often we allow our thoughts to be cluttered with useless worry, and the more we entertain worry, the stronger it grows. For your marriage to be bulletproof, trust must be both vertical (trust in God) and horizontal (trust in your spouse). Contrary to what we may think, God has never failed. We fail, but He does not. Too often we dilute trust with our words and actions and allow our relationships to become compromised. How does this translate into your daily life and marriage? Choose to be mindful of the thoughts you entertain. Do all you can to strengthen your marriage, and God will do the rest.

Numerous times throughout Scripture we are commanded to refrain from worry, but it seems to be a natural part of living. Still, worry destroys trust, depletes energy, and inhibits creativity and growth. Worry will kill the intimacy and passion in your marriage. If you choose to do so, there's plenty you could worry about, but what fruit would that bear? Constant worrying and nagging in your marriage will poison the bond you share and lead to a roommate-like relationship instead of one that is passionate and loving. Refuse to settle for having a marriage that becomes a statistic and invest in your relationship first! Walk in trust with each other and with God, finding empowering affirmations in His Word to reassure yourselves in times of difficulty.

Quick Tip

It may seem like discussing worry together is odd or even worrisome, but if you constantly succumb to worry in your life, you will constantly empower the enemy of fear, worry, and pain to run your marriage. Don't fall into this trap! It is nothing short of self-anguish and torture. You cannot love your spouse wholly until you have a reckless love for God and a healthy love for yourself. Today, know that tolerating worry is destroying your future and keeping your marriage from being the best version of what God intended for you.

Sheepdog

Knowing God's promises gives us peace, but you will, at times, find yourself dealing with issues of trust and worry. Watch the thoughts you entertain and command those things to come into alignment according to the authority of God's Word. Knowing His promises are true and that He never fails, how can you address these common issues in your life? First, realize you will have moments of worry, fear, and distrust. It's when they have become chronic that the issue is serious. When you allow worry, fear, and distrust to take control of your thoughts, your words, and your actions, they become a problem. Today, pray the truth of God's Word over your spouse. Pray with your spouse about the issues of worry and trust.

Spouse

Taking authority over your thoughts means you have recognized something doesn't align with the authority of God's Word. In order to do this, you must know the truth of His Word and how it applies to your life. You don't have to live with worry. You don't have to live in agony or fear all the time. Will there be times these issues arise? Absolutely. But, instead of allowing them to dictate your attitude and behavior, remember today's verse. Give your worries and fears to God, command those thoughts to align with the authority of God's Word, and He will give you peace. Today, pray the truth of God's Word over your marriage.

Questions for Discussion

- What are you worried about today?
- What is the truth God wants you to remember when the enemy puts lies into your mind?

Heavenly Father, thank you for setting us free from the destructive power of worry and giving us the wisdom to seek you. Thank you for teaching us to align our thoughts with your Word and helping us to no longer allow negative emotions to create division in our marriage. Amen.

The Vulnerable Spouse

*What a wretched man I am! Who will rescue me
from this body that is subject to death?*

ROMANS 7:24

There are several studies on the divorce rate among law
enforcement personel, but few are conclusive. Overall, it's estimated
that between 40 and 50 percent of all marriages in America end in
divorce, with subsequent marriages yielding even higher divorce
rates.[2] When comparing divorce rates by the occupation, the
numbers become more confusing. We could fill many pages with
reasons people choose to divorce, and in some cases, justifiably so.
But other than infidelity or abuse, what cause is there? "Forgive
seventy times seven," and then more (Matthew 18:22 KJV). We
are all subject to sin, to failure—even terrible moral failure. That is
why we need Jesus even more! People change and sometimes grow
apart, but marriage requires an ongoing effort, not just on holidays
or when things are at their worst.

Your marriage does have hope. There is a future for holy
marriages, but it requires effort and an appetite for the things of

2 *"Marriage and Divorce,"* American Psychological Association, http://
www.apa.org/topics/divorce.

God. You must be willing to become vulnerable before God with your heart and weaknesses, ask Him to strengthen you, and walk in the abundant strength only He can give. How can your spouse trust you to do anything if you are not willing to admit areas of weakness or vulnerability?

Quick Tip

For some, having the perspective of God as a loving father is a far-fetched fantasy. Maybe you already know the truth, so this will serve as a good reminder: God is not mad at you. He loves you more than you can ever fathom. He is always waiting on you with open arms. Today, take one step toward being vulnerable before God. After all, He already knows your secrets. Open your hands and heart and allow Him to begin weaving His goodness into the fiber of your being.

Sheepdog

When was the last time you woke up and thought, *I want to be average today*. Nobody thinks that! Well, at least no one who accomplishes anything in life thinks that. If you want your marriage to flourish and grow, you will be required to have courage and be vulnerable with your spouse. This is easier to do when you realize the frailty of life and learn to number your days. By nature, you are likely a competitive person or someone who takes great pride in their work. There is a stigma in some parts of society that suggests taking pride in your marriage makes you a weak sheepdog. You are not weak. It's a matter of choice.

Spouse

Ephesians talks about the spiritual armor of God. While all the parts covered are listed in Scripture, there is nothing protecting the backside of the warrior. Everyone has vulnerabilities, but this is the beauty of marriage. You are supposed to protect each other—physically, emotionally, and spiritually through prayer. If this life is going to be great for you, you have to abandon the poisons that tarnish it. As strong as you and your spouse may be, he or she is depending on you to help cover their areas of weakness.

Questions for Discussion

- What is a weakness you have that you want your spouse to protect?
- What is one way you can cover a vulnerable area in your spouse's life today?

Heavenly Father, thank you for covering our marriage with your protection. Thank you for giving us your wisdom and discernment to see and address vulnerabilities in our relationship and for the heart to cover each other in prayer. We thank you for the promises of your Word and ask for your covering in our marriage. Amen.

The Reality of Trust in Marriage

If I could speak all the languages of earth and of angels,
but didn't love others, I would only be a noisy gong
or a clanging cymbal.

1 CORINTHIANS 13:1 NLT

Bill pulled into the driveway at home, grabbed his bags, and
prepared to go inside. His new duty orders weren't changes he was
excited about, and he knew his family would feel the same way.

"Kids, Dad is home! Hey babe—how was your day?"

Everything seemed so perfect today as he walked into his
home, lovingly greeted by Michelle, his wife of eighteen years. Bill
greeted his kids, his wife, and placed his mail and packages on the
counter nearby.

"What's that?" Michelle asked inquisitively.

"Let's talk about it later after we get the kids to bed." Bill
wanted to wait for the perfect time to approach this issue—he knew
it would be tough on Michelle and the kids.

Bill and Michelle represent millions of couples in America
today. Bill chose to enter his home and enjoy peace. He knew that

to keep Michelle and their kids at ease, he needed to communicate his new orders in a proper manner. His approach was motivated out of love, not anger, frustration, or disgust with the new changes. It doesn't matter what you are dealing with. When you are authentically transparent, loving, and sensitive to the feelings of your spouse and children, you will find that trust goes hand in hand with love and communication.

Quick Tip

Trust is established when two people who cannot see all the answers and challenges the future holds choose to talk to each other honestly, openly, and vulnerably, relying on each other through everything. Trust is a silent weapon. In any healthy, happy marriage, trust and love are like two lovers dancing. They can dance alone, and they may do a better job at it alone, but together they create something special. You can love without trust, and you can trust without love, but combine the two in a marriage and you have a very special relationship.

Sheepdog

One of the greatest gifts you can give your spouse is security. By effectively communicating, maintaining trust, and keeping your focus on Christ, both you and your spouse will find a deeper sense of security and intimacy. No matter the changes life throws at you, being intentionally focused on the fundamentals of marriage will always produce life-giving fruit. Doing the work to keep your marriage healthy and thriving isn't always sexy or easy. Sometimes it is even inconvenient and downright difficult. Effort and transparency will be the things your spouse desires to see when it comes to keeping trust healthy and alive in your marriage. Take one step to be more transparent with your spouse today.

Spouse

Taking time to break away from the daily grind and focus on each other is not always an easy thing to do. In a busy world where both spouses are often working more than forty hours per week, a date is more of a fantasy than a reality. But, the less time you spend with your spouse, the more you grow apart. The reality of trust is that is requires effort; it requires you to spend quality time with your spouse, and it requires open, honest, and meaningful communication. Today, do something nice and out of the ordinary for your spouse.

Questions for Discussion

- In what ways does your spouse demonstrate trustworthiness?
- When you're going through a challenge, what can your spouse do to make you feel more secure?

Heavenly Father, thank you for the faith to trust you, and for the courage to trust each other. Neither of us are perfect, but with you at the center of our marriage, we can grow in our relationship with you and with each other. Today we ask your blessing on our trust for each other. Help us keep the trust we have for each other healthy and thriving as we remain committed to you and to each other. Amen.

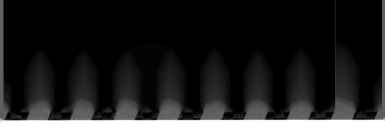

Trust Killers

Human anger does not produce
the righteousness that God desires.

JAMES 1:20

You spend much of your life working to earn the trust of others, but in a single moment it can all be lost. Law enforcement is a zero-defect profession with no room for error, especially in today's society. This level of pressure is one reason staying laser-focused on your marriage and mindful of potential relationship pitfalls is so important. Recognizing the presence of trust killers is paramount. For example, when you are spiritually disobedient to the commands God has given, you invite trust killers into your marriage. Refusing to communicate in a loving and effective manner with your spouse kills trust. Although many trust killers are unrecognizable in the early stages, preemptive strategies can help thwart their influence.

Maybe one or both of you have invited trust killers into your marriage, either knowingly or unknowingly. For example, when things get difficult, do you choose to remain silent, avoid conflict, or keep secrets from each other? Maybe, without the knowledge of your spouse, you choose to talk about your problems with someone else. Or perhaps you quietly struggle with issues of anger or substance abuse. The bottom line is that if it doesn't build or nurture trust between you, it is likely killing your marriage. This doesn't mean either of you should always be on edge about making a mistake, but be aware and conscious of the effects of your actions. Don't get so caught up in the grind of daily living that you lose sight of the beautiful gift God has given you. It's easy to get stuck on autopilot living and forget to nurture your marriage. Take action against trust killers by spending quality time daily with your spouse in prayer.

Quick Tip

Doing the right thing often doesn't come easily. Challenge yourself to be so intensely determined to protect and nurture your marriage that it becomes a daily part of your life. A few trust killers are anger, silence, lust, secrets, lies, and apathy. Aggressively seek to control or eliminate these trust killers in your life. Today, recognize the symptoms and signs of trust killers in your marriage and take the necessary steps to remove them from your life.

Sheepdog

Think about the number of things you do daily without even thinking about it—grooming and hygiene, tying your shoes, blinking—and most of those things happen before you start your day. It's part of your nature. That's why you likely don't give it a second thought before doing it! Do one thing daily to improve your relationship with your spouse, even if that one thing is breaking a bad habit you have or changing something about yourself. Surrendering to your negative emotions and desires will bring temporary satisfaction, but it will cause permanent harm to your marriage. Today, pray with your spouse about eliminating trust killers from your relationship.

Spouse

Marriage isn't a blame game. When things go bad it is often tempting to point fingers. Now is the time to recognize the issues that can lead to deeper problems in the future and address them completely. Instead of sarcasm, speak with sincerity. Instead of subtle slights, speak with love and the grace of God. There's no magic formula to a successful marriage, no secret recipe; it requires both spouses humbly loving, gently serving, and relentlessly pursuing each other. Today, ask your spouse to share with you their thoughts on the presence of trust killers in your marriage. Be realistic and honest. Then pray together for the wisdom to deal with those trust killers.

Questions for Discussion

- What behaviors are trust killers for you?
- What behaviors are trust builders for you?

Heavenly Father, thank you for giving us the ability to recognize the presence of dangerous elements in our marriage. We ask you to give us the wisdom to do our part and for you to remove the trust killers from our lives. Amen.

Day 26

It's a Balancing Act

> Commit everything you do to the LORD.
> Trust him, and he will help you.
>
> PSALM 37:5 NLT

James and Melody were high school sweethearts and had been married for fifteen years. Both of them joined the police academy five years after getting married and were hired right out of the academy at the same department. One recurring issue was the fact that Melody worked night shift while James was assigned to the opposite night shift investigations squad. While they did not have children, this was still a taxing issue on their marriage. They were seeing each other only in passing, and on their days off, they spent time testifying in court. Weekends together were rare, and intimacy had grown cold over the past ten years. Neither spouse was transparent in their communication, and they even held separate bank accounts. The lack of togetherness had caused them to grow apart, and Melody eventually expressed her desire for a divorce.

You may find yourself in a similar position to James and Melody. Maybe you've expressed your desire to call it quits and walk away. The lack of margin in our marriage—whether it is concerning time, finances, or making allowance for each other's faults—creates unnecessary pressure and stress. Addressing issues early on can help your marriage immensely and aid in maintaining healthy communication and trust. When you commit your career to God but fail to commit your marriage to Him, you place your heart in an endeavor that will not last, despite having vowed to remain committed until you die.

Quick Tip

When you're committed to a noble and worthy cause, you may feel compelled to make whatever sacrifices are necessary for the greater good, but this can inadvertently cause you to neglect the marital relationship you vowed to love, honor, and cherish for life. You should be careful to balance work and marriage, never allowing either to become an idol in your life. You cannot commit to God anything you worship other than Him. God's love for us demonstrates the blessing we can find in total surrender to Him. That's the beauty of a relationship with Christ. Remember the vow, "until death do us part"? It wasn't, "until careers do us part." Today, take an inventory of your heart—would you walk away from everything to protect your marriage, faith, and family?

Sheepdog

Balancing career and family is one of the greatest challenges of any sheepdog today. It's not just a balancing act of time but emotions and energy as well. Giving your best on the job is good, it's noble, it's even a worthy cause, but what do you have left to give your spouse? A good work ethic is a positive character trait until it costs you the most precious gift—that of family and marriage. Your career or accomplishments are not worth losing your family and marriage. Don't destroy the trust you have by neglecting to give your spouse the time and attention they deserve. If you don't have quality time together daily, schedule a weekly date night and make it a priority to talk through any pressing issues daily.

Spouse

It is not uncommon for both spouses to work full-time jobs, but not everyone is in the same situation. Mutual appreciation expressed for the sacrifices made to meet your financial obligations can create opportunities for positive engagement between the two of you. Your spouse may not be aware they are giving more of themselves to their career than they are to the marriage, so be careful not to assume it is an intentional or known behavior. Discuss with your spouse if either of you are more committed to your careers than you are to your marriage.

Questions for Discussion

- How much of a priority is your career overall in your life?
- What would you give up if it meant saving your marriage?

Heavenly Father, we thank you for the blessing of having work to do that provides financially for our family. We thank you for the opportunity to serve. Help us never lose sight of our priorities: you, our family, and then careers. Guide us and keep our hearts close to you, directing all we do to honor you above everything else. Amen.

Technically Speaking

"Therefore what God has joined together,
let no one separate."

MARK 10:9

Twenty years ago, having a conversation about smartphones
and marriage would've sounded like a script from a sci-fi movie.
Today, if you and your spouse avoid talking about communicating
transparently, you are setting your marriage up for failure. You
cannot afford to have a prideful or entitled attitude that embraces
the "I am an adult—I can do what I want" philosophy. Instead,
know there are many who have lost their careers, marriages,
and even their freedom because they embraced that faulty line
of thinking. The freedom to communicate at any time across a
multitude of platforms—often anonymously—creates temptations
that exceed the boundaries of marriage. These secrets seldom
remain secrets for long and often have punitive and compounding
consequences.

Your expectations of trust and privacy in your marriage are
only as good as your accountability and transparency with your
spouse. Together you are one entity. If you want complete and total
freedom to do as you wish, it might mean you desire to step outside

the boundaries of safety that God has established. It is for your own benefit that you have absolute openness and transparency with your spouse as it relates to your digital communications. This may mean you willingly provide passwords, usernames, or the security key to access your smartphone. Don't sacrifice the goodness of your marriage for the temporary satisfaction gained from the vain attention of someone else online. It is both proactive and wise to notify your spouse of any communication with a member of the opposite sex.

Quick Tip

Temptations will never go away; instead, they will only increase. Prepare your heart and mind for the moment of greatest temptation. It is wise to seek an exit strategy before those temptations arise and have a healthy conversation with your spouse about the issue. You may not see casual communication with a member of the opposite sex as a threat, but as it develops into friendship, intimacy is inevitably shared, and a breach of trust will likely occur. Openly discuss your expectations related to smartphones and other forms of available digital communication with your spouse.

Sheepdog

There are times and situations when it is simply not safe to relay information to your spouse. It's not a matter of whether they are trustworthy or not; it is simply a matter of security and protocol. Communicating the potential for these situations ahead of time and establishing other accountability measures will aid in reducing any potential conflict that could arise. Establish boundaries, have safeguards in place, and be sure to have effective accountability. Be sure to talk with your spouse today about unconventional situations at work where communication topics may be off-limits.

Spouse

As much as you want to know all the juicy details of your spouse's life while they're on duty, there are times when it is simply not in the best interest of either of you for all the work details to be available. Knowing this truth early on can save you from conflict and personal anguish. Your spouse may want to share every detail with you, but protocol, security measures, or their concern for you may keep them from sharing. Talk with your spouse today about potential limits on the work-related details you're able to share and how to address this issue in your marriage.

Questions for Discussion

- What topics are off-limits for discussion? Why?
- What safeguards could you set in place to protect your marriage from secrecy that could destroy it?

Heavenly Father, thank you for the advancement of technology and what that means for our society, relationships, and business. Today, however, we ask for clear perspective and wisdom regarding communicating with others via text message or over the phone. Help us realize there are no secrets hidden from you, and what we do in private will eventually be revealed in public. Amen.

Breaching Intimacy

> Marriage should be honored by all, and the marriage bed kept pure, for God will judge the adulterer and all the sexually immoral.
>
> HEBREWS 13:4

If you were to sit down with a group of friends or colleagues and have a discussion on what trust, unfaithfulness, and intimacy in marriage looks like, you would have enough to fill a book. The dynamics of life are unchanging, but they look different to every person. Various situations and influencers affect a person's convictions and way of thinking. At the end of the day, do not stray from the standard of God's Word as it relates to these major issues in your marriage. Jesus raised the standard for purity when he said sin begins at the first conception of lust, well before a physical encounter has even occurred (see Matthew 5:28). This places emphasis on the importance of avoiding any action or thought that will breach the intimacy between you and your spouse.

Don't allow exposure to this world's darkest evils to soften your convictions, morals, or conscience. The worst thing you can do is stray from what you believe. Focus your efforts on building, protecting, and nurturing your marriage, and do not allow intrusive relationships to interfere with the intimacy you have built with your spouse. Allow nothing and no one to divide you and your spouse. Your bonds on duty or on the job should never take priority over the bond you have at home. Fight for your marriage. Love your spouse relentlessly, unconditionally, and make them a priority.

Quick Tip

Just before you engage in a dangerous encounter on the job or if something isn't quite right, you'll have a feeling, a moment of intuition. God will guide you through the paths of peril and trouble, but it is up to you to respond and follow His lead. The enemy uses worry and anxiety to dilute and poison the intimacy you have with your heavenly Father. Those same negative emotions can ruin marital intimacy as well. Take action today by surrendering worry, fear, and other negative emotions to God.

Sheepdog

Taking radical action to protect life and limb is something you do daily when you put yourself in harm's way. Take radical action today in your marriage by bringing your relationship with your spouse to God and asking for His divine input through His Word, the Bible. It's not a popular thing to remain faithful, and it may result in you being ostracized among your peers. But at the end of the battle, you will emerge victorious and whole. Honoring and preserving the intimacy you have with God and the marital intimacy you share with your spouse is the most valiant and vigilant thing you can do to protect your marriage.

Spouse

If you want your spouse to talk openly with you, you must first be willing to refrain from responding in a confrontational, judgmental, or accusatory manner. If honestly sharing details about life on duty sparks further distrust, a direct trust issue with your spouse may not be the problem. It could be deep, negative emotions tied to past hurt instead. Talk to your spouse today about one way you can protect the integrity and sacredness of the intimacy you share.

Questions for Discussion

- How would you like your spouse to respond when you share vulnerably?
- What is one way you can protect the integrity and sacredness of the intimacy you share?

Heavenly Father, thank you for showing us the way to walk in this life and the way to honor you. Help us protect the intimacy in our marriage and keep it pure, lively, and growing. Guide our steps and keep our hearts receptive to your convicting power and love. Amen.

Double Lives

The temptations in your life are no different from what others experience. And God is faithful. He will not allow the temptation to be more than you can stand. When you are tempted, he will show you a way out so that you can endure.

1 CORINTHIANS 10:13 NLT

Stories heard on the front lines can unravel the mind and desensitize the soul to the pain and heartache experienced by others. In the same way, justifying actions in response to temptation and minimizing consequences can drive a dagger into the heart of a marriage. Rest assured, the things you do in secret, in the dark, will be made known in public. There will come a time when you will answer for your response to temptation. When that time comes, will you be found trustworthy, or will you have left a trail of broken promises?

Everyone has their own vices, and not all of them lead to destructive behavior in marriage. Your vice may be food or time alone, but too much of anything can be unhealthy. Perhaps it is pornography, gambling, or alcohol. There are many dynamic elements in the battle for holiness and righteousness, but you must remember that Jesus paid the price and won the battle. Christ's sacrifice means victory over temptation is possible. Avoid justifying your actions and minimizing the consequences, which are the first steps toward succumbing to temptation. Instead, walk in the confidence you have in Christ and look to Him for help when temptation comes.

Quick Tip

Your response to temptation will determine how well you steward your spouse's trust. If you succumb to temptation, it doesn't have to be the end of your story. The key to a successful response to temptation is having a plan in place ahead of time, before the moment arises. Maybe you are tempted to quit on your marriage, or to give in to old habits. Today, talk with each other about creating a single-step plan to deal with temptation.

Sheepdog

If someone was attacking you, you would not pause to think through the process of responding, making sure you could justify your decisions in the moment before you leapt into action. It would be too late. No, if you were actively being assaulted, you would respond violently, aggressively, and with extreme hostility. My fellow warriors, temptations in life are created to lure you to your own death. Resist them violently. Do not negotiate. Instead, fight for your marriage and do not let up until you achieve victory. Today, pray with your spouse about responding to temptation on duty.

Spouse

Your marriage will fail if you try to defeat every attack with your own power and strength. At some point, you must realize the power to be victorious isn't your own. Rather, it resides in you as a believer through His Word and through His Spirit. Temptation spans many issues and areas of life, but justifying your wrong actions can lead to devastating consequences. Start fresh today with your spouse and mark the occasion—draw a line in the sand, circle the date on the calendar, or renew your vows. Whatever you do, agree to battle temptations together as a team through the available power of the Holy Spirit. Talk with your spouse about creating a plan to address temptation, both individually and together.

Questions for Discussion

- What is your biggest area of temptation at home or at work?
- How can your spouse support you in this area so that it does not overcome you?

Heavenly Father, we thank you for your mercy in creating a way out of situations where temptations are present. We know there is no area of our life where temptation will not present itself, so we ask for your wisdom today—wisdom to create a plan and discernment to see the path you have created for us to avoid temptations and defeat them. Amen.

A Trail to Trust

Those who are loved by God, let his love continually pour from you to one another, because God is love. Everyone who loves is fathered by God and experiences an intimate knowledge of him. The one who doesn't love has yet to know God, for God is love.

1 JOHN 4:7-8 TPT

Life isn't the result of a single action. You cannot take one breath and live for many years. The miracle of life, with its numerous processes and events, is complex and beautiful. Marriage is similar. You cannot exchange vows one day and live happily ever after with no further action. Your marriage requires daily breathing—a daily exchange of vows through action and trust. There are perils and dangers, but it is an adventure you must take with your spouse hand in hand, fighting for each other, not fighting against each other. Every action you take, every response to adversity, is an opportunity to either build trust in your marriage or chip away at the trust of your spouse.

You have the choice between cultivating trust with your spouse and enriching your marriage, or creating problems for yourself and pain for your spouse. Be intentional with your actions and think before you speak. Don't be apathetic or careless about protecting your spouse and your relationship. Everything you do today results from your beliefs and thoughts, so be careful what you entertain in your mind. This will translate into better conversations and actions, leading to more desirable outcomes in the future. Strive today to create a habit of building on trust each day. Be authentic. Be pure. Seek God.

Quick Tip

A trail will lead either to a known or unknown destination or circle back to where you began. You do not know what the future holds, but you can take the right actions today by creating positive, sustainable, healthy habits in your marriage. These habits will help create more predictable and positive outcomes in the future. Write down one habit you can cultivate today that will improve your marital journey.

Sheepdog

Routine can be deadly, unless that routine is sustainable and necessary for life. Think about routine behaviors like taking a step or blinking. You can perform those actions without even thinking consciously about them. In the same way, routine in your marriage is not a matter of becoming complacent but building positive muscle memory. Getting strong physically is great, but if your marriage is weak, you will be weak.

Spouse

What will you take on the trail to trust? Will you take past hurt? Anger? Resentment? Unforgiveness? Take only that which you need. Take also plenty of forgiveness, as you'll use it often—offering it freely to others and dispensing it to yourself. Take an abundance of love. Pack plenty of patience. Temper your expectations and don't expect to reach your destination of trust immediately—it's a journey of growing closer with every intentional step toward reaching your goal. Every action you take can have a profoundly positive impact on improving your marriage. Act with kindness and love, being generous with forgiveness.

Questions for Discussion

- What is one thing you can build into your marriage muscle memory today?
- What is one thing you can contribute on the trail to trust with your spouse?

Heavenly Father, thank you for your unending supply of forgiveness and grace. Thank you for loving us and for placing us together as husband and wife. We are deeply grateful for the relationship we have and ask you to guide our steps on the trail to trust—helping us grow deeper with you and each other. Amen.

The Fate of Your Marriage

"For I know the plans I have for you," says the Lord.
"They are plans for good and not for disaster,
to give you a future and a hope."

JEREMIAH 29:11 NLT

The past several days you've focused on fostering a solid foundation
for trust, restoring trust, and taking the necessary action to protect
the trust you've established in your marriage. But what is the fate of
your marriage without trust? It is destined to be miserable, full of
conflict, and likely to end in heartbreak and disaster. If you choose
to please only yourself and get your own way, you choose to trust
only what you know and your own path. God's plan for your life
and your marriage is to give you a future and a hope; they are good
plans, but we must trust them. Trust is woven throughout our lives
and is a critical component of a successful marriage.

It's a matter of choice, not a matter of personal rights. You
choose to either build a healthy marriage with trust or you choose to
take actions that destroy that trust. It's a matter of accepting personal
responsibility for your own actions. The fate of your marriage is
in both your hands—yours and your spouse's. Choose love and
forgiveness. Choose to fight for your marriage and for each other,

eliminating those voices that would create conflict and division. If choosing to protect and nurture marriage isolates you from some, so be it. The health of your marriage relationship is important and not something to be taken lightly. Declare the promise of Jeremiah 29:11 over your marriage and relationship today.

Quick Tip

One of the best things you can do in your life is to study the Bible, know its promises, declare those promises over your spouse and marriage, and then act upon those promises. When we think, talk, and act contrary to God's plan of hope and goodness for our lives, we create our own conflict. There are enough challenges in life without creating our own issues. Don't place your sights on a perfect marriage; place your sights on a healthy, growing, thriving marriage. Place your sights on treating each other in a way that is good and honorable to God.

Sheepdog

You do not trust what you do not know or give attention to. Spend quality time with your spouse and make them a priority. God spoke His plan of a future, hope, and goodness over you. Now you should speak His word into your marriage. It's not something weird to declare His truth and promises for your family, it's biblical. Today, speak His blessings over your marriage.

Spouse

From the day you said "I do," you began a journey with your spouse that will span an entire lifetime. Sadly, many journeys end in divorce, but that doesn't have to be your outcome. By keeping Christ at the center of your marriage and doing the right things together and for each other, you will soon enjoy the fruit of God's plan for your life. Perhaps things have been unbearable and divorce has been on the table as a real option. Choose to step into hope and love, walking into the future of God's abundant promises for your marriage today. Choose one thing you can do today to be good to your spouse.

Questions for Discussion

- What is something your spouse does that you appreciate?
- Why do you think God brought you together as a couple in marriage?

Heavenly Father, thank you for showing us the importance of trust in our marriage and how to nurture trust for a fruitful relationship. We declare your word from Jeremiah 29:11 over our marriage, our future together, our family, and our finances. We know you have good for us, and we accept it with open arms. Amen.

Conflict Resolution

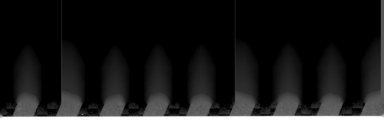

Pray Before Engaging

"I also tell you this: If two of you agree here on earth concerning anything you ask, my Father in heaven will do it for you. For where two or three gather together as my followers, I am there among them."

MATTHEW 18:19-20 NLT

A moment of conflict can be a great opportunity for us to experience the presence of God and see His grace amplified and alive. However, when you attempt to navigate conflict with your own understanding, it is impossible to please God and find a viable end to the issue. Praying together with your spouse before addressing conflict in your marriage prompts you to resign your own desires and will to the purpose and plan of God for your marriage. Your heart and mind will become more aligned with and sensitive to the leading of the Holy Spirit.

Ask God for His direction, wisdom, and leading through conflict. You shouldn't be deceived into thinking marriage will be without conflict or challenge—that would be foolish. Instead, prepare ahead of time. Whatever the conflict is about, you should always proceed with prudence and love, extending grace to your spouse. The power of God is present and available for your marriage today. The Holy Spirit dwells within you as a believer in Christ, and you have been given the tools you need to navigate difficult times. Address conflict with precision, stay on topic, honor God, and love your spouse through it all. When you choose to take these steps with your spouse before conflict arises, you are teaming up to demonstrate obedience and faith in Christ and His living Word. You can be sure He will honor that!

Quick Tip

It is not necessary to have a clear understanding of every piece of the issue you are in conflict over. It is necessary, however, to proceed with prayer and grace. When you are reluctant to pray about an issue, it's probably an indicator that you really need to pray about that issue. The most important element of having a bulletproof marriage is being able to successfully and lovingly navigate conflict together. Today, discuss one way you can prepare for potential future conflict now.

Sheepdog

What is the cost of peace? It is the willingness of brave men and women like yourself to face the most dangerous threats to our way of life. It is someone willing to confront the issue and eliminate the threat. No one respects someone who loses their temper—especially if it is a leader. Don't be the one who loses their temper in the midst of conflict. Navigating conflict in marriage requires precision communication techniques. Control the emotional side of your tone and address the issue with love. Write down one thing you can do to prepare for conflict in marriage and pray with your spouse about it.

Spouse

If you have resentment in your heart toward your spouse, you will be reluctant to pray with them about anything, much less an issue causing conflict in your marriage. Open your hands and your heart and let God deal with it. Don't diminish His role in your life by attempting to deal with pain yourself. Preparing for conflict in marriage means being willing to work through any and all problems together. Today, pray with your spouse even if you are mad at them.

Questions for Discussion

- In what way does prayer change things for the good?
- What is one way you can overcome divisiveness to achieve peace in your marriage?

Heavenly Father, thank you for your Word and for the instructions you give us. We ask you to help us navigate conflict in our marriage in a way that honors you and reflects our love for each other. Amen.

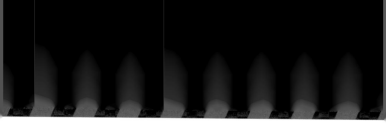

No Counterattack

The teachings of hypocrites can destroy you,
but revelation knowledge will rescue the righteous.

PROVERBS 11:9 TPT

"You're just as stupid as your family, John. All you had to do was tell them you didn't want to be transferred, and I am sure they would have let you be. I don't know why I married you!"

Rebecca was known for her temper, and this wasn't the first time her anger threatened the future of their marriage. They were great together until something threw them off-balance. Then they resorted to hurling spiteful words and personally attacking each other, which led to deep, lasting pain. Rebecca allowed her emotions to take the reins and produce words she would regret for many years to come.

What good are your talents, your gifts, and your blessings, if you lack love? The threat of peace to your home is rooted in subtle acts of hatred and seeds of discord. To counteract this means placing a higher priority on intentionally showing the love of God to your spouse, even if you are verbally attacked or offended. You know the importance of fighting fair and doing it all in love, but when your spouse uses hurtful words or actions toward you, responding with equal force is not the answer. It may sound elementary at this point, but name-calling is not a fruitful and productive way to accomplish anything in marriage. It only creates more division and resentment! Whatever you do in your marriage must first be packaged, sealed, and delivered with love.

Quick Tip

Jesus said to turn the other cheek. This is not permission to be a doormat and allow others to physically or verbally assault you. Rather, it is a command to let Him be the avenger of your injustices. It means you let go of the feelings of resentment and forgive quickly. Never permit ongoing abuse, but if it is a situation that can be resolved, do everything in your power to address it. Today, resolve with your spouse that counterattacks are no longer an option for your marriage. Agree and promise to fight fairly, lovingly, graciously, and selflessly.

Sheepdog

You are a sheepdog—protector, guardian, and warrior. But you are also a human being with emotions. When exposed to some of the worst garbage in this world, your emotions can affect you in terrible ways if you aren't prepared. You might inadvertently take those emotions out on your spouse through expressions of anger and resentment. Strive to be loving, gentle, and kind with your spouse. Instead of responding with anger or counterattacks, respond with love, be patient, and use self-control. Don't allow your emotions to dictate your words and cause you to sin in anger. Conflict can arise at any moment, but you don't have to be blindsided. You can keep your eyes open and be prepared for what may come. Pray today with your spouse about fighting fair and navigating tense emotional situations together with grace.

Spouse

Saying hurtful things may not cause your warrior spouse to break down and cry, but it will leave a mark, and there will be consequences. Even your sheepdog is human, contrary to what they may think at times, or even what you may think. Often their emotions are buried under layers of hurt, shame, and guilt, and it will take time to get to the vulnerable heart of your spouse. Counterattacks in a disagreement or conflict create a foothold for the enemy to slide in and infiltrate your marriage. This type of behavior is not honoring to God, nor does it align with His nature. Let all you say and do be dripping with the love of God.

Questions for Discussion
- What does fighting fair look like to you?
- What character qualities does God want you to demonstrate when conflict comes up?

Heavenly Father, thank you for teaching us that conflict is not to be avoided but navigated with the grace and love you've given us. Guide our hands, feet, mind, and bodies to think, live, speak, and do in ways that will eternally honor and glorify you. Amen.

Healthy Minds Think Alike

For God has not given us a spirit of fear and timidity,
but of power, love, and self-discipline.

2 TIMOTHY 1:7 NLT

Fear often paralyzes and prevents any type of action, leading to a breakdown in communication. If you assume your spouse knows something, but they're not communicating with you, you may become fearful about what you perceive has gone unspoken. The consequences of not talking with your spouse can include useless and avoidable arguments for that reason. Consider a fictional couple and their finances. If each assumes the other is going to pay the electric bill and neither remits the payment, they end up with no power and a moment primed for volatile conflict in the home.

Sometimes a simple question presented in kindness for the sake of clarity can prevent and remedy any issues that may be festering. This is not to say you should not have deep and meaningful discussions often, but don't neglect the little things—they can add up to major issues over time if not addressed. You may think you know what your spouse is thinking, but do not assume you are on the same page all the time. Open up, talk, and, most importantly, listen to your spouse. Listen to how they are feeling and work together in unison on all issues as a couple. Finding common ground may seem impossible, but through the power of compromise and communication, you can address any expectations that have not been clearly discussed.

Quick Tip

Some of the greatest weapons the enemy uses against your marriage are assumptions and expectations that are not clearly communicated. These assumptions create unfounded thoughts that lead to time-consuming, useless, pointless arguments. The life of your marriage is found in many veins, but one of the primary avenues is through unity and communication. Be sure you make a solid effort to remedy any miscommunications with each other today. You cannot achieve unity without communication. What assumptions in your marriage can you address and clarify today?

Sheepdog

Don't allow your call to serve act as a disrupter in your marital communications. Long after your career has ended, you will still be married. This is the primary call in your life as a married person—to minister to, serve, honor, love, and cherish your spouse and family. Talk to your spouse about one assumption you may have today and open a clear line of communication.

Spouse

What may be a simple issue can lead to a highly contested conflict if not addressed. Having regular discussions about finances, parenting, plans, or other issues in your marriage can help thwart any potential conflict. Spend some time today talking with your spouse about any possible assumptions that could lead to future conflict.

Questions for Discussion

- What assumptions or expectations do you have in your marriage?
- What unspoken expectations have led to misunderstandings?

Heavenly Father, thank you for the gifts of wisdom and a sound mind and for showing us the truth about communicating in our marriage. We ask you to help us see the little issues and address them right away instead of allowing them to go unnoticed and unaddressed. We know you will open our eyes to any seed of the enemy in our home so we can be victorious in our efforts. Amen.

Addressing Anger

In your anger do not sin. Do not let the sun go down
while you are still angry.

EPHESIANS 4:26

When you're on duty and someone is fighting you, you know you
are protected by law in doing what is necessary to meet the level of
force necessary to subdue them. Using punitive force out of anger
or lack of control means you will face severe consequences. This
goes for law enforcement, first responders, and members of the
armed forces. You know your rights when you're facing a combative
subject. But you also know there is no room for emotional
retaliation on the scene. For example, if someone is drunk and
disorderly and non-threatening, you are not going to intentionally
or maliciously use lethal force. If there is no threat, there is no
force. Anger, if not bridled and controlled, can cause you to make
decisions that will cost you your career, your license to serve, your
family, your peace, and your reputation.

It's not a sin to be angry. In fact, it's perfectly normal to be
angry. The sin is created in your response to anger. Your spouse will
make you angry, but do not punish your spouse in anger, creating
a situation where addressing conflict becomes nearly impossible

and creates division in your marriage. Allowing your emotions to override your self-control, self-discipline, and love for your spouse will also critically damage the trust your spouse has for you. The only way you can restore your spouse's respect and trust after an angry outburst is to apologize and be vulnerable with them. Being vulnerable destroys the shame anger causes and brings true healing and intimacy to your marriage.

Quick Tip

One of the greatest antidotes to anger is patience and love. When used properly, these two virtuous elements can help calm emotions and tempers, reduce any blowback from anger, and aid in navigating volatile situations. When you are angry, remember that God's Word says it's okay to be angry as long as you do not sin in your anger.

Sheepdog

When the potential for retribution is removed, anger loses its power. There is no anger when we understand our citizenship is in heaven and our rights are governed by the kingdom of God. Selfishness leads to deep anger, which leads to broken homes. Find the trigger to your anger—perhaps it is something that has repeatedly irritated you or caused you to become hostile. Find the trigger and pray with your spouse regarding this issue. The fruit of anger is never sweet. Instead it leads to death and destruction.

Spouse

No one wants to be in a relationship where hostility is present and peace is absent. Anger, if not addressed, can destabilize your marriage. What you may perceive as irrelevant and minor may be a major trigger to your spouse. In fact, what attracted you to your spouse in the beginning may now be a major annoyance to you.

Superficial conversations will not lead to a discovery of deep-rooted triggers of negative emotional issues. You must be willing to dig deep, ask the hard questions, and implore God to reveal these things to you. At times, it may require the assistance of outside help. Talk with your spouse and pray about the things that trigger anger in your life.

Questions for Discussion

- What is a primary trigger of anger in your life?
- What is one way you can work on eliminating or preventing anger from ruining your marriage?

Heavenly Father, thank you for our marriage and a home that is filled with peace. We ask for your hand to move in our lives and reveal to us the triggers of our anger. Remind us when we are angry to lean on your promises and not on our own understanding. Amen.

Anger Management

A hot-tempered person starts fights;
a cool-tempered person stops them.

PROVERBS 15:18 NLT

You are called to be a peacemaker—to end fights, resolve conflict, address evil, and work for good to prevail. This is impossible if you cannot effectively manage your emotions, including anger. Failure to manage emotions can have serious consequences. Hot-tempered people have lost jobs, careers, families, and even their own freedom. When you realize that patience and love, while difficult to master, are the answer to defeating a bad temper, you are set free from the bondage of runaway emotions. Don't allow circumstances in your marriage to dictate your emotions—you are in control of those things. It is no one else's power, place, or responsibility to initiate, trigger, or control your emotions. That power and responsibility is yours alone.

Not being able to manage anger or a bad temper is a sign of emotional and spiritual immaturity. Everyone has their breaking point, but being quick to anger about every little issue is an uncalled-for and destructive behavior. Your ability to control your temper will determine the depth of intimacy you experience with God and your spouse. It will also be a determining factor in the amount of favor you experience with God. These destructive behaviors destroy any potential for healthy conflict resolution and can lead to broken homes and lives. Instead of being quick to anger or hot-tempered, practice patience with those you love dearly.

Quick Tip

Have a controlled discussion with your spouse about addressing or preventing future temper rampages. Be aware of your triggers and typical responses and acknowledge that they are likely different than your spouse's. The single greatest thing you can do in your marriage today is to empty your heart of the reasons to be angry and fill your heart with the knowledge that God is love instead. Work to control your emotions now to avoid future damage to your relationships and marriage. Allow God to guide you to a path of healing from negative emotions and behaviors. Work today to help each other navigate these changes, and support each other as old habits are replaced with God's design for your marriage.

Sheepdog

A temperamental person is the greatest threat to effective conflict resolution. Your decision to remain loving, kind, and gentle can mean the difference between having a peaceful resolution to conflict or a digression in your marriage. Effort is required on your part, but if you choose to take the proper step of simply remembering what God's Word says about the issue and applying it to your life, you will have enough time to consciously decide to put your temper to rest. You can resolve conflict with a cool head, but a hot temper will escalate the issue.

Spouse

There are things in your life that will be triggers to frustration, anger, and impatience. Maybe it is a process of whispering a quick, simple prayer when you are frustrated or upset that helps you get through. Whatever your method, remember those feelings will not last, but the consequences of a bad temper can last forever. A seed sown in frustration can lead to contention and strife. Work together with your spouse to navigate through emotional times, especially when you are both frustrated and temperamental.

Questions for Discussion

- What is one way you can navigate through emotional issues in your marriage while keeping your cool?
- What is one way your spouse can help you de-escalate a hot temper?

Heavenly Father, help us remain cool-tempered in all our situations, especially in the midst of addressing conflict. We do not want to dishonor you and create division and hostility in our marriage by being hot-tempered. Thank you for your blessings and wisdom in our marriage. Amen.

Remember the Goal

Make every effort to keep the unity of the Spirit
through the bond of peace.

EPHESIANS 4:3

Brian was facing an uphill battle toward a full recovery, having been shot in the line of duty. He found himself battling deep depression and regular nightmares in which he relived the call that changed his life. Michelle, Brian's wife of nearly twenty years, had never dealt with anything like this before. It was a situation they had always known was possible, but they had never thought it would happen to them. Soon, Brian had withdrawn from communicating, slept all the time, and was drinking excessive amounts of alcohol. He was facing a major career change as he was no longer able to serve as a law enforcement officer. This is where their marriage was forged in excellence. Michelle didn't become irate, hateful, nagging, or impatient with her husband. Though it was uncomfortable for her, she did all she could to help him. They sought professional help, worked together, and soon it wasn't just Brian fighting the battle alone; they were fighting the battle together, hand in hand.

Your careers, parents, children, finances—anything in life can drive a wedge between you and your spouse if you don't covenant together to live life from a position of unity. You are one team. Period. There's no fighting to defeat your spouse in anything; you face each battle as a single unit. This may seem odd to those who have only known division and conflict in their relationships. But this is a new day, and this is the best way. How do you live life, address conflict, and enjoy a sense of togetherness? By regularly practicing humility and patience, gentleness and love; by favoring your spouse before yourself and tolerating zero selfishness. Maybe you think this sounds impossible. But it is not impossible. It is very doable, and it is the only way you will achieve victory and have a bulletproof marriage.

Quick Tip

Know your limits and when you've achieved all you can together without assistance. This is where professional guidance comes in. There are many trained counselors, therapists, and teams of people who can help your marriage. Draw the line today. What is the breaking point for your marriage? When will you seek help in order to work together? Consider annual marriage counseling or an annual marriage retreat to keep your bond healthy and tight.

Sheepdog

You will never be stronger than your ability to accept and receive help. Your spouse is your greatest asset, most reliable teammate, strongest ally, and best companion. Don't discount the ability of someone you may perceive as a less qualified individual to help you break through difficult situations. Be willing to accept their help, and be willing to give them a hand when they need it too. Often the desire for help in marriage is not vocalized—break the mold and be willing to ask for help. Never be afraid to speak up and tell your spouse or anyone else that you need assistance with an issue. Pray and ask God to reveal ways your spouse can help you today.

Spouse

No matter the struggles either of you face, step in and help each other through life's challenging moments. Nothing can separate you if you will be intensely focused on doing the things God directs you to do in His Word, keeping your heart pure, and protecting the unity of your marriage. Your job may not always involve danger or life-and-death decisions, but you are an integral part of your sheepdog's life. You need each other desperately.

Questions for Discussion

- How can your spouse help you today?
- What is one way you can promote the mission of "one team" in your marriage today?

Heavenly Father, when things seem to be falling apart in our marriage, remind us that no matter what happens, we are on the same team—one marriage, two people, one heart, one God. We seek to honor you, and we choose to work together toward a more unified marriage. Amen.

Establish Boundaries

Have nothing to do with sexual immorality, lust, or greed—
for you are his holy ones and let no one be able to accuse
you of them in any form.

EPHESIANS 5:3 TPT

When Jason began his career in law enforcement, he and his wife, Angie, had been married for six months. This was new territory for them. In their short time together, neither of them had ever spent an extensive amount of time away from each other—not even during the dating phase of their relationship. Interference from outside relationships had never been a problem, until one evening when Angie saw Jason's phone light up with messages, one after another.

"Who is texting you, Jason?" Angie wanted to know. "Why are there pictures of another woman on your phone?"

After lying initially, Jason admitted to having an inappropriate relationship with a coworker.

"She listens to me Angie. You have no idea what I deal with daily. She just gets me. Why is that a problem? I'm not having sex with her."

In Jason's mind, unfaithfulness to his wife was set within the boundaries of the bedroom. It didn't include the emotional intimacy he shared with another woman. Even though Jason admitted to never having a physical relationship with his coworker, unfaithfulness crept in when he chose to place his trust in another woman outside his marriage. Maybe you have experienced similar issues in your marriage. It's time to establish healthy boundaries and cut ties with the relationships that are causing interference. No mercy, no justifying, no compromise. If it crosses a boundary you've set for your marriage, it's got to go.

Quick Tip

Maybe this sounds like old-fashioned, outdated advice, but if you want to protect your marriage from outside threats and position your relationship to not only survive life's challenges but to thrive, you must become relentless and tenacious when dealing with threats. When it comes to boundaries in your marriage, don't give in to the theory of grey areas. Set clear boundaries, and then adhere to them. Don't back down. Don't be afraid. In what area of your marriage do you need to draw new boundaries today?

Sheepdog

Your marriage will not be like everyone else's marriage. Don't compare the boundaries of another relationship to the boundaries in your marriage. You know what your spouse will find as unfaithful or a breach of trust. If you are unsure, ask your spouse today. Don't leave this part of your life to assumption. The standard of intimacy and trust may seem to be a sliding scale in society, but the standard established by God has never changed. Before sin ever becomes a manifested act or behavior, it is fulfilled in the heart. Perhaps you will find concerns around boundaries in parenting, communicating with the opposite sex, dealing with the in-laws, or even finances. Get a clear picture of what your marriage boundaries are and live within them. You'll be glad you did.

Spouse

While you may hear other spouses talking about how they do things in their home, those same behaviors may not be effective in your marriage. Discovering how God's Word and the principles of a bulletproof marriage apply to your life may mean you give up more things, relationships, or time to make it work in your home. Spend time today talking to your spouse about areas of your marriage that need attention as it relates to boundaries. Your approach will be unique from anyone else's, but remember, you are on the same team, not opponents.

Questions for Discussion

- What are some healthy boundaries for your marriage?
- What constitutes a violation of those boundaries and how do you address any violations?

Heavenly Father, thank you for the wisdom to create boundaries in our marriage. We recognize that every person requires boundaries and limitations for their own safety and well-being. Help us clearly define and adhere to the boundaries you have established for us. Amen.

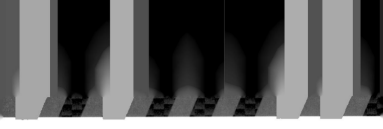

No Matter What

With tender humility and quiet patience, always demonstrate
gentleness and generous love toward one another, especially
toward those who may try your patience.

EPHESIANS 4:2 TPT

Gentleness, quietness, and tenderness are all qualities that may
often be confused with shutting down or withdrawing. Living under
constant scrutiny as a first responder or member of the armed
forces will take a toll on your marriage and other relationships
if you succumb to a cynical attitude and allow it to harden your
heart. Other negative personality traits may also develop. While
it is difficult to keep a tender heart toward those you love, it is not
impossible. When we lean on our relationship with Jesus rather than
our own strength and efforts, it is more than possible.

For some, understanding the balance that's required to live the
life of a sheepdog entails making significant adjustments, and that
may be the case for you. It may mean you need to have a discussion
with each other as a married couple about how you will cope with,
unload, and unpack those negative and toxic things you experience
daily on duty. No matter what you do, remain gentle and generous
with your love toward each other. Remain humble and kind. There

will be days you will try each other's patience, but take a breath and remember that you are in this journey together. Your marriage is a safe place for you to rest, recharge, and refocus.

Quick Tip

Jesus never said, "I will love you as long as you do not do (fill in the blank)." He promised an unconditional, unwavering love. Even in your mess, He loves you with a gentle, kind, and generous love. Work to emulate that love to each other in your marriage. You will certainly face many challenges—some may even seem overwhelming—but serving God together in unity will make you victorious. Pray specifically for God to protect your hearts as you walk through life so you will always remain tender, kind, loving, and generous—especially toward Him and toward each other.

Sheepdog

One day your life will be easier, but today is not that day. Today is a day of preparation. It may be a day where you must act in excellence to apprehend evil or restore order. At the end of the day, however, your spouse is not your adversary. No matter how others treat you on the job, remember to demonstrate unconditional, unwavering, and unrelenting love to your spouse. Operate as one team, one unit, with one focused mission. When you are weak, talk to your spouse.

Spouse

Unfortunately, we live in a society that deems kind, gentle, and loving warriors as weak. They are labeled as vulnerable and often ostracized by their peers. Reinforce the fact that your spouse can be both a mighty warrior and a loving, gentle spouse. Support them as they seek to find that balance. Finding the time to talk to each other is great, but there may be times your greatest gift will be to listen to your spouse. Allow them space to be vulnerable. This will keep the ground of their hearts tender and tilled, soft and prepared for the seed of God's Word.

Questions for Discussion

- What is one thing you can do to protect the heart of your spouse so you can continue to grow as a couple?
- What is one way you can help foster a healthy attitude in your spouse?

Heavenly Father, thank you for your lovingkindness in our marriage as you have so many times demonstrated your compassion in our lives. We ask you to help us remain tenderhearted toward you, your Word, the leading of your Spirit, and each other. Help us recognize when it is time to ask for help! Amen.

Marriage Remix

For the believing wife brings holiness to her marriage,
and the believing husband brings holiness to his marriage.
Otherwise, your children would not be holy,
but now they are holy.

1 CORINTHIANS 7:14 NLT

Traditions vary from one family to the next, depending on your upbringing, culture, location, and beliefs. Some may not have had a faith-based upbringing, and if your spouse is a lifelong believer, this can present unique challenges if it's not addressed with love. Your spouse likely has many things in common with you, but if you don't see eye to eye on faith in Christ, it can make for divisive and confrontational discussions. However, don't discount what you can give to your spouse in spiritual leadership. You both have something to contribute to your marriage, no matter how insignificant it may seem.

You could take today's Scripture and look at it from various theological perspectives, but at the end of the day, whether or not you and your spouse are both believers, the presence of Christ in your home will make a tremendous difference. Your children will see Christ in you—in the way you love your spouse, in the way you handle conflict—and it will be evident to them that you are a changed person. Instead of being frustrated with the presence of conflict, accept it as a challenge to grow closer in your relationship with Jesus. Everything you endure—whether conflict or peace—will push you closer to Christ.

Quick Tip

Your united approach to conflict will be a dynamically empowering element when it comes to finding a peaceful resolution together. Never allow any conflict to push you apart as a couple; rather, find common ground or a way to get closer and learn to compromise and negotiate with each other. Some people may suggest that differences in people create conflict and potential for disaster in marriage, but those differences are what make your marriage beautiful and full of potential. Don't allow another's perspective about marriage to create conflict. You both have something to offer each other, and that makes your marriage perfectly imperfect.

Sheepdog

Instead of focusing on the value you present to your marriage, look at the value your spouse presents. Gratitude takes us a long way down the road of life—especially in marriage—and it can do wonders to quiet discontentment and poor communication. Gratitude also helps you to see more of the good your spouse does in your relationship, among a myriad of other health benefits.

Spouse

It takes zero effort to talk negatively about your spouse, to complain all the time, and to do all the wrong things in life. It's a natural flow to go with your own selfish desires and live an unbridled life. But there is no good fruit in that! It takes work to do the right things in order to reap an eternal reward. Your perspective of your spouse can be drastically changed today through expressing gratitude for the contributions your spouse makes to your marriage. No matter how seemingly insignificant those contributions may be, express your heartfelt thanks for all he or she does. What are some ways you can express a grateful heart for all your spouse contributes to your relationship?

Questions for Discussion

- What are some things you are grateful your spouse contributes to your marriage?
- What are some ways you can express a grateful heart that are meaningful to your spouse?

Heavenly Father, we thank you for the revelation knowledge of your Word, and the fact that you have given each of us unique personalities, gifts, and skills that make the world a better place. Help us see the value in each other's differences rather than the negative aspects of those differences. May our hearts always be grateful for all you have done but also for what we do for each other in our marriage. Amen.

Avoid Belittling

It is foolish to belittle one's neighbor;
a sensible person keeps quiet.

PROVERBS 11:12 NLT

After a series of unpleasant exchanges of yelling, cursing, and name-calling, Rich and Melinda retired to separate rooms in their home. The previous six years of their marriage had been tumultuous to say the least, and things were starting to get serious. After three miscarriages, Melinda felt like she was the problem or that she had done something God was punishing her for, and Rich wasn't helping the cause any.

"You are the one who is at fault, Melinda!" he yelled. "Everybody told you not to smoke, but you didn't listen and you never took care of yourself. Look at you!"

He was demonstrating the behavior of a man void of all wisdom, and he certainly didn't talk to Melinda like he had any love in his heart for her.

Belittling others is often a symptom of unaddressed pain from the past that only creates new pain for others. Another translation of Proverbs 11:12 (NASB) says, "He who despises his neighbor lacks sense." Don't despise your spouse, no matter how painful the circumstances. Draw close to each other through intimate communication, intense worship, and consistent pursuit of the Father. The heart is unable to lie and will reveal the deepest, most sincere motives, feelings, and intentions. If your heart is not pure and hungry for the presence and Word of God, you will cause yourself and your spouse deep pain. Don't belittle your spouse in the home, and definitely not behind their back.

Quick Tip

The underlying issue behind belittling your spouse (or anyone else) is an inability to control your anger. The tendency to belittle others is indicative of someone who is lacking in some area of their emotions or ability to communicate properly. It doesn't mean you are a bad spouse. It's just a sign that you're in need of God's healing touch in your life. Before you cross the line of belittling your spouse or calling them names, take time to think about what you are going to say and ask yourself, *Will this honor God?* and *Will this nurture love in my marriage?* If you cannot answer yes to both of those questions, don't say it.

Sheepdog

If you participate in name-calling, belittling, or being critical of your spouse, examine your own life. What is it that you have left unaddressed? Maybe you have thick skin and don't see the error in your ways, but be sensitive to how your spouse receives your words. Consider teaming up with your spouse to record the next interaction you have with them for reference. Don't try to sneak it into the conversation, but use it as a tool to see, from a different perspective, how you talk to each other. You don't need a talk show host to send a film crew into your home to record your daily life to save your marriage. You can do this on your own.

Spouse

Most men wouldn't admit it if you were belittling them, but over time, it will create resentment in them and conflict in your marriage. Resentment, anger issues, or other underlying emotional issues are often the reason someone belittles their spouse. If you've been guilty of this in the past, why not apologize for that behavior specifically? Call it by name. Don't leave that wound to fester. If you are the recipient of this type of abuse, when things are calm and peaceful, let your spouse know those type of words hurt you and you will not tolerate it.

Questions for Discussion

- How have you unknowingly (or knowingly) belittled your spouse in the past? Apologize to your spouse for this.
- What is one way you can create a loving exchange of words in your marriage, even during conflict?

Heavenly Father, we come to you as a married couple asking for healing from any previous pain we've caused each other through belittling. We ask you to help us find healing in your Word and Spirit for any underlying issues causing this type of behavior. Amen.

Don't Be Stupid

The fear of the LORD is the beginning of knowledge,
but fools despise wisdom and instruction.

PROVERBS 1:7 NKJV

Over the past sixteen years, Steve had worked with his agency
full-time while volunteering as a firefighter in his small community.
Recently, his wife had noticed he wasn't sleeping through the night
and was waking up with nightmares. Steve's mood had become
unstable, and he was irritable more often. He never wanted to talk
to anyone about what was going on or what had triggered these
behaviors, but he was showing all the signs of someone in serious
need of help. Steve suffered in silence, refusing to get help out
of fear—fear of rebuttal from his agency and colleagues, fear of
losing his job, and fear of what his family and spouse might think.
Eventually, Steve's supervisors called him in for a meeting and
required him to seek counseling.

Had his supervisors not picked up on Steve's subtle signs
of distress and not taken the repeated calls from his family and
friends seriously, who knows where he would have ended up. More
importantly though, Steve did the work, took the counseling and
instructions he was given to heart, and is now a changed man. It

didn't happen overnight and it wasn't easy, but he did it. When you refuse to accept and adhere to good instruction, counsel, or even correction, you put yourself and others in jeopardy. Refusing to accept help is not a sign of strength; it's a sign of immaturity. It doesn't matter what anyone else thinks—humility and living from a place of holy reverence for God will lead to a long and fruitful life. Don't reject godly counsel.

Quick Tip

Do not try to parent your spouse. That will only create resentment and dishonor in your marriage. Do listen to anyone who is trying to help keep you from danger, harm, or sin—including your spouse. You may be blind to your own path of foolishness, so listen to those God will place in your life to help you find your way back on track. Give a discerning ear to those who love and care about you when they offer good wisdom, counsel, and instruction.

Sheepdog

Guard your heart against pride, and don't let it rob you of the best part of life. Give heed to the advice, correction, and counsel of those who care about you. It's not always someone trying to "be all up in your business," as it may well be the best thing for you at the time. If your spouse pleads for you to listen, then listen. They may see something—a danger or threat—you may be blind to. A wise person discerns good counsel and instruction and welcomes correction. You don't have to be ruled by your emotions, circumstances, or the triggers in your life. You can take control and help your spouse navigate these issues as well.

Spouse

Be wary of dismissing the advice of others or silencing the conviction of the Holy Spirit in your life. When you choose to step over the conviction of God, avoid His instruction and counsel, and ignore correction, you willingly walk into trouble. These self-inflicted wounds could be avoided. Just as your spouse looks out for your well-being, look out for your spouse. When trying to persuade your spouse to heed your counsel, do so in a loving way—not as a parent would a child.

Questions for Discussion

- What is one way your spouse can help you avoid relational dangers?
- What is one way you can look out for your spouse today?

Heavenly Father, thank you for correction, instruction, and the counsel of godly people in our lives. Thank you for hearts that heed good, godly counsel and correction. Thank you that our hearts remain soft and tender toward you as we heed the conviction of your Spirit. Let us embrace correction and counsel and honor you in all we do. Amen.

Bridled Emotions

The wise are cautious and avoid danger;
fools plunge ahead with reckless confidence.
Short-tempered people do foolish things,
and schemers are hated.

PROVERBS 14:16–17 NLT

Marital conflict comes in many forms and often at the most inconvenient times. As a couple who is committed to Christ and keeping Him at the center of your marriage, remember that you will likely face spiritual battles. There will be times when you see others who are not living a life after the heart of God, seemingly skipping through life with no troubles. Don't let this discourage you. Instead, resolve to keep your peace during challenging times. Your spouse is not the enemy, no matter what anyone else may say or what you may think. When you run recklessly into conflict with no plan, no strategy, and no weapons to counter the enemy, you are being foolish. It is just like being short-tempered with your spouse—you're just using your energy to battle yourself, which is not fruitful or productive.

Instead of doing foolish things in the heat of conflict, choose to use wisdom. Use the same emotional management skills you use in conflict on duty, but remember, your spouse is not your enemy, and you are not fighting against each other. You are fighting for each other. Bridle your emotions; don't let them control you. Control the words you say and the way you say them or else the circumstances that result from foolish, short-tempered reactions will control you long-term. Typically, sheepdogs do not avoid danger. They confront it armed, prepared, and ready to attack instead. Engaging with your spouse with unbridled emotions is reckless and will result in deep pain, consequences, and resentment in your marriage.

Quick Tip

Unaddressed underlying issues can often be the result of someone who has unbridled anger, bitterness, and lack of control over their emotions. As a sheepdog and the spouse of a sheepdog, it is necessary to look for the warning signs of issues that need your attention. Do not tolerate verbal, emotional, or physical abuse. If your spouse needs help, help them seek it out. The Word of God is still the single greatest salve for a broken man or woman.

Sheepdog

Determine now what is more important to you—a moment of temporary reprieve gained from releasing unbridled emotions or the peace found in using wisdom, patience, and longsuffering. Guilt is the fruit of losing your temper, and pain is the price your spouse pays. If you are difficult to live with, is it because you have allowed past issues to go unforgiven? If your spouse is difficult to live with, is it because of past negative situations? Treat your spouse like your heavenly Father is present in your conversations, because He is. You wouldn't allow someone to dishonor your spouse with any type of abuse, just as the Father will not allow you to continue in those behaviors. If this hasn't been an issue in your marriage, how can you protect your relationship falling prey to it in the future? Today, talk with your spouse about any unaddressed issues that may be creating division and conflict between you.

Spouse

Sometimes, the best strategy to diffuse a person who is emotionally unbridled is to ignore their actions. There are other times, however, when those actions must be addressed. In any case, don't discount the possibility that you or your spouse may need assistance. Seeking professional counseling is not a negative thing, and it may help reveal deep underlying issues that would benefit you both if addressed.

Questions for Discussion

- What do you feel is the best way to respond to a short-tempered person?
- How can you speak to your spouse with peace and love?

Heavenly Father, we thank you for the self-control, self-discipline, and wisdom to keep our emotions in check and speak to each other in love. Help us honor you and our relationship in the way we respond to conflict and adversity in our marriage. Amen.

Commit to Fight Fair

The tongue has the power of life and death,
and those who love it will eat its fruit.

PROVERBS 18:21

Here's a secret you may not already know: You are going to have disagreements and, sometimes, all-out fights in marriage. Gasp! Who knew? It's no secret if you've been married any length of time, since you know your spouse's quirks and how badly they can get on your nerves. Keep in mind that your words can do more harm in a moment of anger and lack of self-control than you could ever imagine. The power of life and death is in your words, so fight fair. Don't cross the line, stay on point, and do not belittle your spouse. Name-calling should have been left in your childhood—there's no place for it in marriage. Agree with your spouse today that you will not allow any part of foolish name-calling in your marriage!

It may be tempting to bring up past issues during a marital battle, but do not do it. Stick with the original issue, keep your voices controlled and calm, and show honor toward your spouse. The words you speak in a moment of anger will bear harvest for many years to come and can severely damage the trust and respect you have developed in your marriage. The moment you think you won't be the one to do something like this will be the moment you become the primary aggressor in a fight. Pride will sneak up and suck the life right out of your marriage. Protect it by addressing conflict with humility and grace.

Quick Tip

Whatever you do, don't make things worse by losing your temper! If you abandon your marriage now because things aren't easy, how many more relationships will you have to go through before you learn how to stick it out in the hard times? Let's be real about fighting in marriage—we're all guilty of doing it wrong. You're going to have fights; just be sure that you fight fair and always hold your spouse when it's all over.

Sheepdog

If you've had a history of not fighting fair with your spouse, there's hope! Today can be a new day. As you fill your heart and mind with the truth of God's Word, submit yourself to the leading of the Great Shepherd, and seek His direction in partnership with your spouse. You will find a massive change taking place in your heart. In a single moment of emotional abandon, you can ruin the respect and trust you once shared with your spouse. It takes a lifetime to earn it and sometimes just as long to repair it when damaged. Don't allow past negative interactions to overshadow the positive potential of the future.

Spouse

Establish a baseline of what you both expect when disagreements and arguments arise. Draw a line in the sand today and jointly vow to never cross that line in your marriage. Respect each other, love each other, and honor each other even in moments of disagreement. Don't allow assumptions and past behavior to dictate how you handle future conflict in your marriage. You're now armed with the truth of God's Word and the ability to lean on His Holy Spirit to guide you through all adversity.

Questions for Discussion

- What are the foundational principles you believe are necessary for a fair fight?
- What is one way you can fight fair with your spouse?

Heavenly Father, thank you for showing us how to rightfully navigate conflict and disagreements in our marriage. We desire to honor you with all we do, even in the midst of trying times. Today we ask that you would help us speak in a loving and respectful manner when we talk with each other. Help us draw nearer to you, Lord. Amen.

Up Close and Personal

Therefore encourage one another and build each other up, just as in fact you are doing.

1 THESSALONIANS 5:11

"I'm not sure how long I can keep doing this, Charlotte. I'm so tired. I'm sick of seeing all the hate and dealing with all the politics and garbage we have to endure. I don't see what good I am doing."

Ronald found himself in a position he swore, as a rookie, he would never get into. He had become hardened by the things of his career, and it had taken a toll on him mentally, physically, emotionally, and spiritually. His time in the field had begun to affect his marriage and relationship with his children.

"Ron, please listen to me. You do more good in a day than most people do in their entire lives. You are a good man, Ron. You are a good husband, a great father, and we adore you. Maybe it is time for you to take a break. Why don't we get the kids together and take a weekend trip away? You've got some time built up, don't you?"

If you find yourself in a similar situation at some point in life, you and your spouse should have an open line of authentic communication that allows room for venting and healing, as

Ronald and Charlotte did. It took courage for him to speak up, and it took a degree of courage for Charlotte to encourage her husband to keep the faith and stay in the fight. Sometimes conflict doesn't look like a fight on the outside. Rather, one or both of you are battling an internal conflict that can be alleviated by encouragement from the other. Today, speak the life-giving Word of God into the circumstances you are facing and encourage each other.

Quick Tip

The Greek word for "encourage" is *parakaleó*, which means, "make a call." What a wonderful way to support each other in times of trouble. Don't be afraid to call to your spouse for assistance when you are dealing with something difficult. Choose to lean on your spouse in troubled times and don't seek other outlets in unfruitful places.

Sheepdog

You may feel like asking for help or desiring encouragement makes you weak, but it doesn't. It's a reminder that, no matter how heroic your actions, you are still a human being comprised of flesh and blood. It's not a sign of weakness; it's realizing your limitations and a reminder that you depend on the help God gives. He will often use the gifts of your spouse to fulfill your needs. Asking for help and encouragement means being vulnerable with your spouse; it means picking the phone up or saying during an embrace, "Babe, I am down. Will you help me?"

Spouse

Your spouse may be excellent at hiding discouragement, but you can observe the warning signs of a sheepdog who is wounded. You may notice subtle changes, but you are armed with a mighty weapon—the ability to encourage. Never settle for a passive answer of "I'm ok" if your gut is telling you otherwise. If you can't get to the truth, initiate the Encouragement Protocol immediately. Begin speaking life into the soul of your sheepdog, creating an environment where they know without a doubt that your arms are a safe place—a place where they can let go of emotional baggage and you have their back, no matter what.

Questions for Discussion

- What is one way you can reassure your spouse that you are a safe place for them?
- What is one way you can not only encourage your spouse today but also be open to encouragement as well?

Heavenly Father, thank you for the gift and ability to encourage one another and to worship you amid life's circumstances. We ask you to help us recognize each other's need for encouragement and discern the right things to say at the appointed time. Amen.

Stay on Point

Some people make cutting remarks,
but the words of the wise bring healing.

PROVERBS 12:18 NLT

Several scientific studies have calculated the number of thoughts an adult human being has per day. Some suggest this number to be as high as fifty to seventy thousand. I bet you didn't even realize you could think that much! Many of these thoughts occur subconciously and escape our awareness. Additionally, it has been recorded that the majority of our thoughts are inherently negative. This means you must submit yourself fully to the power of God's Word and its ability to renew your mind as you meditate on the truth found in Scripture. Address the root of these negative thoughts, and you will begin to see a shift in your thinking process.

While your brain is the most fascinating organ in existence, multitasking limits your excellence in any one area. This means that during marital conflict, you should focus on one issue at a time. When you attempt to address multiple issues in one argument, you will find your blood pressure, stress level, and temper rising to meet the frustration. This is a toxic mix and can be detrimental to resolving conflict. Today, should you and your spouse find yourselves in a verbal argument, stick to one point. Don't give in to the temptation to tackle multiple unrelated issues.

Quick Tip

Maybe you've heard the common saying "I can only help one person a day, and today isn't your day." While you can actually help more than one person per day, you cannot fully give your attention to more than one issue at a time. Multitasking is often touted as a positive and desirable trait in business, but it is a negative element in marital communications. Listen to what your spouse is saying, and then respond in a way that expresses your love, care, affection, and respect. During your moments of external or internal conflict, stay on point. Keep your focus. Don't allow raw emotion to determine your response.

Sheepdog

Resentment can often come knocking when you are angry and engaged in an argument. It presents itself when we allow the seeds of our emotions to flourish into negative words instead of speaking from a controlled tongue. Your spouse desperately needs you to control your emotions and the words you say. The pain of attacking him or her during an argument does not easily heal and can make the future tumultuous. When you find yourself getting off point— attacking your spouse with your words and negative emotions— remember the toll it takes. When you are engaging in conversation with your spouse and emotions are high, whatever the situation, keep your focus and keep the center of your discussion bound in love and honor.

Spouse

As you peruse through photographs of memories with your spouse, are there certain pictures that cause you to have negative feelings? Are there pictures that remind you of fights or long nights apart? Or are there pictures that remind you of blissful days together where you enjoyed each other's company? What you do today with your spouse will be a memory tomorrow and long into your future together. Previous arguments don't have to determine the direction of future arguments. Work together. Prepare in peace for moments of conflict and walk in love. Don't allow temporary emotions to sow permanent roots into the heart of your marriage.

Questions for Discussion

- What is something you appreciate about your spouse?
- Which of your spouse's talents or traits is the most supportive to you when you are down?

Heavenly Father, thank you for the wisdom to stay focused in conflict. Help us keep our eyes on you and not the negative things that come up in our lives. Grant us the peace to walk calmly through the den of lions and overcome negative emotions with the presence of your Holy Spirit. Amen.

SECTION FOUR

The Intimacy Initiative

On the Same Page

Anxiety weighs down the heart, but a kind word cheers it up.

PROVERBS 12:25

By reading this devotional daily, you have been taking steps to improve your intellectual intimacy with each other. Reading a book together can increase intimacy in your relationship. Different studies suggesting the reason Christians divorce as often as other religious or non-religious persons vary, but the common theme is that committed relationships fall apart when the sanctity of marriage isn't embraced equally by both husband and wife. Maybe Christian divorce rates remain on par with non-religious couples because many Christian couples only worship together at church one day a week. It goes back to the whole "form of religion without power" thing. For whatever reason, Christians lack the staying power when they should be leading the pack.

Do you feel it is impossible for you to read the Bible with your spouse every day? If so, don't focus on reading several chapters; just spend time each day reading together. Spend time each day praying together too. It's not about being rigid in your daily routine—it's about placing the priority on committing your life to each other and to God, no matter what. Society offers a long list of possible

153

reasons to divorce, but at the end of the day, if you are married, fight to stay married. A powerful ally in the fight for marriage is time together. Choose to spend some of that time together reading the Bible or other books and praying daily.

Quick Tip

The single greatest game changer in your life is the Word of God, but it is no good to your life if you do not read it. Reading the Bible together, studying it, and asking God to let those words take root in your heart will give you a lasting marriage. Faith comes by hearing, and hearing comes by the Word of God. If you want to increase your measure of faith, read the Word and practice it. There is no greater way to build your bond of intimacy and friendship as a married couple than to spend time studying the Bible, praying, and worshiping together. Commit to spend time reading the Bible to help you on your journey together.

Sheepdog

Building a solid foundation for lasting intimacy in your marriage doesn't have to be mundane or boring—it can be an adventure you take together that causes you to flourish and grow! The spiritual intimacy between you and your spouse is the fundamental intimacy needed for the other areas of your life to flourish. It is paramount for you to take the lead and work with your spouse to deepen your faith in Christ, together. Have a conversation with your spouse about current events or a topic from the Bible and discuss it together. This bonding of intellects can lead to richer and fuller days of enjoyment, just as it can also help you grow deeper as friends.

Spouse

When was the last time your mind was stimulated by a movie, book, work of art, song, or conversation? Serve as the stimuli for your spouse's intellectual journey. Some say the couple who plays together stays together, and while that is true, it is also true that the couple who learns together, stays together.

Questions for Discussion

- What are some ways you can connect with your spouse intellectually?
- What is something you've been thinking a lot about lately that you can share with your spouse?

Heavenly Father, thank you for the insight and knowledge to identify the building blocks of intimacy in our marriage. We ask you to guide us to the things we have in common that will connect us more deeply to each other and you as we grow intellectually together. Amen.

According to the Same Beat

Let everything you say be good and helpful, so that your words will be an encouragement to those who hear them.

EPHESIANS 4:29 NLT

Maintaining a consistent and effective level of intimacy in marriage requires one special element: mutual effort. It is unlikely you both like the same music all the time, but you may have a special song that brings back memories of your dating years. Make an effort to find the things you both enjoy, but avoid picking up unwholesome habits and behaviors. Consider the things you watch on television or listen to on the radio. Maybe a book you're reading, while enjoyable, does not result in growth or a profitable soul. Remember that whatever you take in through your eyes and ears comes back out in the form of words and actions.

What unwholesome things do you need to cut from your marriage today? Today's verse tells us to avoid foul or abusive language because it is unwholesome and does not encourage the hearer. Only you know if you and your spouse are walking in sync, living in step with one another. If one special song can generate so many fond memories for you as a couple, think of what your marriage could be like if you were constantly living according to the same beat. This whole life is like a dance—a series of negotiations, compromises, and embraces. But like every song and dance, this life will also end. Choose to live life to the fullest with your spouse.

Quick Tip

You know spontaneity can be good for your marriage, but spontaneity in music is only good if all the musicians are playing the same song. Is there a song with special meaning to your marriage? Likely you've even danced to it a time or two (together, of course!). Dancing together is a great excuse to hold your spouse close and one of the best ways to learn to live in step with each other. Before this day ends, grab your spouse by the hand and dance. It doesn't have to be perfect or competition-worthy—just dance together.

Sheepdog

A demonstrated, worthy, and intentional effort to improve the intimacy in your marriage without shooting straight for sex can do wonders for your marriage. Take your spouse for dance lessons. Learn something new together. Grab her hand when she's not expecting it and dance in your home. Don't fall into the rut of being destroyed by boredom and routines.

Spouse

Finding ways to be creative and keep your marriage thriving means effort from both of you. Don't be afraid to dig up those special songs and dance together. If your spouse has been reluctant to have fun with you, please do not criticize their dance skills. Enjoy the time together. Revive the passionate relationship you once had by living according to the same beat and getting in the groove together as a team. Grab your spouse by the hand and dance, even if there is no music.

Questions for Discussion

- What is one way you can show effort to improve the intimacy in your marriage?
- What is one of your favorite memories of your spouse doing something special to show love to you?

Heavenly Father, thank you for the gift of marriage. Help us never miss the opportunity to embrace each other, dance, kiss, and express our love for each other. Help us honor and glorify you with our marriage today and every day. As we seek to draw closer to you, we ask you to bless our marriage with a strong, intimate bond that is unaffected by the things of this world. Bulletproof our marriage. Amen.

Road Trip

My lover said to me, "Rise up, my darling!
Come away with me, my fair one!"

SONG OF SOLOMON 2:10 NLT

Changing the scenery can be good for your marriage. Consider taking a day trip or planning an impromptu weekend getaway. Either way, your time away doesn't have to be extravagant, expensive, or burdensome. Take the time while you are away to reconnect with your spouse. If you will be traveling by automobile, plan some conversation topics beforehand so you do not sit in silence for the duration of your trip. Make a list of things you want to discuss and share them with your spouse before you leave. Taking time away with each other can allow you the opportunity to reconnect and have fun together.

Numerous times in the Song of Solomon there are invitations from both the lover and the beloved. This expression of desire is one of the overlooked and underappreciated elements of a bulletproof marriage. Desire for your spouse—desire to spend time together and to enjoy each other's company—builds intimacy. With the presence of chronic stress in your lives, these times away together are invaluable. What is equally important is your expressed desire for each other. These expressions of desire can prove especially beneficial to your marital intimacy. While it may be a step outside your comfort zone to express desire for your spouse if your marriage has grown cold, it is a step of faith. God will honor your faith and reward your obedience as you follow His lead.

Quick Tip

What are some of your favorite getaway spots? Maybe you enjoy the beach life, mountains, or a good hike together. Request vacation time, find a place you both want to visit, and then make it happen. Your time away together can provide opportunities for fruitful conversation and connection. If you haven't been away together lately, it may be time to plan a trip together. Today, list three potential destinations you can visit with your beloved.

Sheepdog

Expressing your desire for your beloved can be one of the most intimate forms of demonstrated love in marriage. Let your spouse know your desire to be with him or her. Let them know you want to spend time alone to simply enjoy each other's company—not just in the bedroom, at dinner, or without kids. Your spouse is your companion, not your competition. Your challenge today is to invite your beloved to run away with you on a quiet getaway, and then overwhelm him or her with goodness and kindness.

Spouse

If your beloved expresses an invitation to go away on a trip together, try to avoid giving all the reasons the plan may fail. Show a mutual effort and respond to the invitation. Maybe the timing isn't right or finances are a concern, but waiting for the perfect opportunity to get away together will mean it never happens. Do you have a seed of desire in your heart to be with your beloved?

Then, as Christ has fully expressed His desire for a relationship with His bride, the church, respond to the invitation your beloved has given you.

Questions for Discussion

- What have been some of your favorite places to go as a couple?
- Where are three places you've never visited before that you would love to get away to with your spouse?

Heavenly Father, thank you for the gift of effort, the will to keep pursuing you and to continue pursuing each other as husband and wife. Stir in our hearts a fresh passion for your Word and help us never take each other for granted. Amen.

Becoming One

Confess your sins to each other and pray for each other
so that you may be healed. The prayer of a righteous person
is powerful and effective.

JAMES 5:16

There used to be a time in America when couples went into their
marriages with an absolute resolve to be married to each other until
death. Now, many list the reasons they will abandon the relationship
before they ever begin! The moment you begin listing ultimatums is
the moment you start punching holes in your own marriage. It will
sink before you can even set sail! Stop giving yourself an excuse for a
way out and start pursuing the Father together. The only hope for a
successful marriage is a joint effort and unrelenting determination to
make your relationship the best it can be. Do the work, do the right
things, avoid the temptation to criticize and dogpile on your spouse,
and seek guidance through prayer.

While most Americans claim to believe in God in some
form or fashion, they admit to not praying daily. The ultimate
key to a successful marriage relationship is daily pursuing God
together with your spouse. Life will get busy and stress will become
overwhelming at times, but as long as the relationship is prioritized

and Christ remains at the center, you will be empowered to overcome any challenge you face together. Beyond all the rules and requirements religion places on mankind, an authentic, intimate, and consistent relationship with Jesus Christ is the single greatest element of any marriage. One way you can get there from wherever you are in life today is to pray. Pray together, pray regularly, pray in the Spirit, and pray boldly.

Quick Tip

Praying together creates an invisible shield of protection around your marriage. It's a secret weapon that cannot be touched, regulated, or controlled by anyone but you. If your prayers have not been answered, consider your relationship with your spouse. Treat your spouse with love, honor, and respect, and God will open the windows of heaven over your relationship. Pray together daily.

Sheepdog

There are many sheepdogs who know the greatest strength they have is found by submitting to the Great Shepherd. We get to know the Great Shepherd through regular prayer, a right heart, pure motives, and studying His Word. Praying with your spouse is a simple yet powerful way to invite God's presence into your marriage. Pray protection, wisdom, peace, and the blessings of God's Word over your spouse. Pray together and individually. This is one area of your life where ammo shortage will never be an issue. You are always fully loaded and ready to pray.

Spouse

The days are busy, jam-packed with things to do and places to go, with no time for peace, rest, or moments with those you love. When you do get time together, you're both exhausted mentally, physically, and emotionally. Communication is often weak and undesirable. However, it's hard to fight each other when you are praying together. One of the most powerful things you can do is to not only pray together but to also pray for your spouse when you are apart. Let them know you are praying for them. Write it down in a journal and watch how God moves in your lives over time. Pray with and for your spouse daily.

Questions for Discussion

- What are you thankful to God for today?
- What is a concern you want to bring to God in prayer today?

Heavenly Father, we come to you as husband and wife, asking you to stir in our hearts a deeper, more passionate hunger for your Word and presence in our lives and increase our desire to pray together more consistently. Would you stir our hearts today not just for each other but for you? Thank you, Father, for this marriage and all you are doing in our lives. Amen.

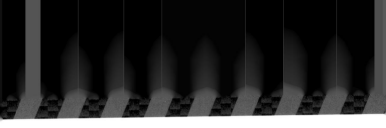

Breaking Bread

And let us not neglect our meeting together,
as some people do, but encourage one another,
especially now that the day of his return is drawing near.

HEBREWS 10:25 NLT

More than 200 billion dollars will be spent on physical buildings in America this year for people to gather and worship God. But at the end of the day, you are the house of God—you are the indwelling place of His presence. No building or sanctuary can contain His presence or do the work He has called you to do. So while it is good and fruitful to gather with other like-minded believers, that should never be the only place you worship together, nor should it be the primary source of your spiritual nutrition. That is one of the greatest reasons so many struggle today! The power of God's Spirit is found in relationship with Him, just as true success in your marriage is found in intimate relationship with each other.

While placing an emphasis on gathering together as Scripture instructs, Christians have forsaken emphasizing the importance of establishing a personal relationship with Christ. There is without a doubt a need for the community of saints to gather, worship together, and encourage each other, but these weekly gatherings should not be your sole source of spiritual nourishment. Pursue together daily study, prayer, and worship. The blessings of God should be a consequence of our relationship with Him, not a primary focus. When you worship with your church community, doing so in one accord as a couple, you will find great strength, encouragement, and prolonged steadfastness. You were never created to live life alone, and your marriage needs community support too.

Quick Tip

It is not uncommon for a sheepdog to have an odd schedule that often prevents them from attending a worship service with their spouse. Many times these men and women have a strong desire to be with their spouse in worship but cannot due to their commitment to serve. Don't take for granted the opportunities you are given to worship together, whether privately or in corporate services. Cherish those times, even if you have different views on the church, pastor, or preaching. The simple act of being together and the unity created from worshiping as a couple can provide tremendous strength, insight, and yearning for God in your marriage.

Sheepdog

You may have an issue with crowds or even attending a church where people you have met professionally are present, but don't focus on the excuses that prevent you from attending church with your spouse. Instead, look at the benefits of worshiping together! It's another opportunity to be encouraged and challenged by other like-minded believers. If you aren't placing a priority on worshiping together regularly, today is a great day to start.

Spouse

Nagging is tiring, counterproductive, and creates an atmosphere for conflict. The best way to love your spouse if he or she is not interested in going to church with you is to always leave the door open for them to attend. Don't be hateful or nag, but rather, create opportunities where they would want to attend with you. Ask God to give you the wisdom and discernment to address this issue in the best way. Never threaten to divorce your spouse just because he or she doesn't want to attend church with you.

Questions for Discussion

- What are some good reasons to attend church together?
- How can you encourage each other to attend corporate worship together?

Heavenly Father, thank you for the freedom to worship you in public and in our home, both individually and as a couple. Help us see the true power of worship and gathering with other like-minded believers. Amen.

Surprise Dates

*Whether you eat or drink, live your life in a way
that glorifies and honors God.*

1 CORINTHIANS 10:31 TPT

Michelle picked up her phone and saw a text message from her husband, Javier. It read, "Be home at 1800. Kids are taken care of. Don't ask questions. Dress nice. Love you." After reading the text, her hands began to sweat a little bit as she was anxious about what Javier meant. *Surely this isn't a date. I wonder if something is wrong. Did he get promoted?* were just a few of the thoughts that ran through Michelle's mind.

"Okay. Anything I need to know about?" she texted in reply.

Javier had planned a nice dinner near the coast for the two of them and an evening away from the daily grind. Once Michelle discovered his plot, her anxiety disappeared, and her heart began to race with excitement and anticipation for their time together.

There are times when you simply cannot surprise a spouse. They are either too good at discovering the secrets, or their anxiety leading up to the date would ultimately ruin the endeavor. If you can pull off a surprise date with your spouse, it is extremely rewarding and you will not regret it! Take time to get away with your lover and enjoy each other's company and companionship. Don't talk about bills, parenting, or anything related to your daily life. Dream together, fantasize together, and plan your future together. Surprise dates are good because they don't allow either of you the time to overthink the evening! Just get away and have fun.

Quick Tip

Men, whether you know it or not, your spouse *longs* for you to pursue her, date her, pamper her, and place her on a pedestal. She may never tell you this, but oh, the rewards you can experience in your marriage! One of the best pieces of advice ever given was by a couple who had been married over sixty years: "Never stop having fun, and never stop having sex." Add to that, never stop dating each other, forgive quickly, kiss and make up and your future together will be a lifetime of joy and blessing.

Sheepdog

Your assignment, should you choose to accept it, is to locate a new restaurant your spouse will love—something that would require you to interact together and doesn't involve staring at a screen for two hours—and plan the date. Don't let him or her know what you are up to, and don't do it today since they will likely read this with you! Pick a day, schedule the date, and sweep your spouse off their feet!

Spouse

It will be difficult, but if your spouse is asking certain questions or sends you a text like Michelle received, go with the flow. Let your spouse take the initiative; let them pamper, spoil, and cherish you. Don't ruin it by saying, "I hate surprises." Enjoy your time together, and don't let age interfere with your desire to have fun and live life to the fullest. Maintaining spontaneity in your marriage will keep it fresh, lively, and exciting.

Questions for Discussion

- What is your favorite memory from when you were dating?
- If you were to have a dream date with your spouse, where would you like to go?

Heavenly Father, thank you for giving us the freedom to enjoy life, have fun, and live our lives to the fullest while honoring you. Grant us the ability to be creative and keep our marriage fun and enjoyable! Amen.

Spontaneous Getaway

Adam and his wife were both naked, and they felt no shame.

GENESIS 2:25

It's time to have some pre-apple garden moments together. Be
vulnerable, be adventurous, and run away together for a getaway.
It's time to go to your favorite vacation spot, have absolutely no
plans, and spend it together doing whatever comes up. Have fun,
enjoy each other, stay up late, sleep in, do things you never do
during the regular grind of life. Don't allow your relationship
to grow stagnant and boring! Surprise each other! Even if it is a
"staycation" and you just send the kids away to a friend's house
or to visit grandparents. Get creative, but most of all, keep things
spontaneous. When you look back on your life in twenty years, you
don't want to look back with regrets. You should do adventurous
things together, go to new places, eat at new restaurants, enjoy
your time together, and you'll be pleasantly surprised at how God
refreshes, revives, and energizes you both.

One thing you will bring back from your getaway together is
perspective. You will begin to see how life should be enjoyed when
you live it without worry, fear, doubt, stress, or anxiety. Taking a
surprise getaway may not always be feasible, so plan surprise dates

by taking the initiative to arrange for childcare, make reservations at a nice restaurant, and have things ready to go. Stop assuming the other spouse *should* be the one to pursue you. Take initiative and light the fire.

Quick Tip

Write down three reasons you can't run away together for a weekend. Likely your list includes time off from work, finances, and childcare. These issues can all be addressed with proper planning and creativity. The trip doesn't have to be extravagant and costly. Do what you have to do to make this happen, and do it more than once every five years. Have a conversation about your dream getaway and brainstorm ways to make it happen.

Sheepdog

Having a spontaneous getaway as a first responder or member of the military may take some extensive planning on your part, which sort of eliminates the whole spontaneous element of the getaway for you. Don't allow the amount of planning involved to keep you from making those plans. The time away together will be refreshing, enjoyable, and provide an opportunity for you both to unwind and relax.

Spouse

If you get the opportunity to get away with your spouse on a short trip, don't let the responsibilities at home cause you to feel guilty or shamed. Enjoy your time together and rediscover a fresh, passionate desire for your spouse. Take the time to renew your spirit through studying the Word, prayer, and worship. These little trips can serve as great breathers in your life together and can help restore your marriage to a healthy and fruitful state.

Questions for Discussion

- What do you enjoy about your spouse?
- If you could pick one place that is within your ability both financially and logistically to travel to, where would you go?

Heavenly Father, thank you for the gift of time together with each other. We ask you to be with us as we spend time together. Help renew intimacy between us and stir our hearts afresh for you. Amen.

Enjoy the Ride

Live happily with the woman you love through all the
meaningless days of life that God has given you under the
sun. The wife God gives you is your reward for all your
earthly toil.

ECCLESIASTES 9:9 NLT

Ray looked at his wife, Susan, as she walked across their living
room, and something about that moment made him deeply grateful
for her presence in his life.

"Have I told you how much I adore you? I want you to know how
much I care about you, and how much I appreciate you supporting,
encouraging, and loving me. Words are inadequate when I try to tell
you how I feel about you." He ended his adoration in a warm embrace.

"Oh, babe, I couldn't imagine a day without you in my life. I
am thankful for you too," she replied.

There are times when the only thing you can do in life is hold
on to God and each other while you wait on Him to deliver you
from difficult times. It's not always an easy journey—or even a
pleasant one—but having a spouse who loves you and cares about
you is a great reward.

When you think about your marriage from this perspective, it causes you to view your spouse in a different manner. For one, you will no longer see them as a burden or nuisance, as you may have in the past. You'll see each other as God intended, and it may even feel too good to be true! When God restores a relationship, He doesn't do it halfway—He restores it to pristine condition, and both spouses must work diligently to keep it that way. Don't look at your spouse as anything short of a precious reward, gift, and treasure from the Father. It will not only help keep things in perspective when you face difficult times, but it will also make the intimacy you share more intense, sweet, and enduring.

Quick Tip

Think about the last time you enjoyed each other's company, had fun together, or complimented one another. You don't mistreat a reward—you cherish it, put it in a special place, and protect it. Treat each other in the same manner and intimacy will begin to flourish!

Sheepdog

If you receive a medal of commendation for your actions on duty, it is often given at a formal ceremony where your actions and character are celebrated. Once the ceremony is over, the medal is placed in a position of honor in your home or workplace. Treat your spouse with great respect and honor, and put him or her on a pedestal above the rest of the people in your life. Show your spouse that they are clearly number one on your list of priorities! Fight for your spouse. Defend, protect, cherish, and adore them on a regular basis.

Spouse

You should never feel ashamed, guilty, or awkward when your spouse wants to adore you. In fact, if more married couples treated each other like the precious gifts from God they truly are, this world would be a sweeter place! Don't let parenting, finances, or other interests drive a wedge in your marriage relationship. Always place the rewards from God ahead of the burdens of this world.

Questions for Discussion

- Why is your spouse God's best gift to you?
- What is one meaningful way your spouse can communicate honor to you?

Heavenly Father, thank you for the gift of our relationship. We are grateful you loved us enough to place us on this journey together. We ask that you would ignite a fresh intimacy and renew our passions for each other as we pursue you and honor each other. Amen.

Budget Boredom

If you have not handled the riches of this world with integrity, why should you be trusted with the eternal treasures of the spiritual world?

LUKE 16:11 TPT

The topic of finances is often intimidating. Although it will be tough, having a budget as a first responder or military family is possible. The thought of a family budget can be just as intimidating as a gaping wound on your body that you don't want to look at— you know it's bad, immediately fear the worst, and just don't want to know the reality of it. If your finances have taken a backseat to other conversations with your spouse, that is a red flag. You should both be involved, aware, and responsible. Taking time daily, weekly, or monthly to discuss your budget can give you more room for planning, giving, retirement, or even leisure.

You will find that as you remain committed and consistent with a budget, your appetite for useless and frivolous things will dissipate. Riches are useless if you cannot manage them. If you don't have a budget remotely laid out for your finances, consider looking into the budget process provided by Dave Ramsey. His courses and books are invaluable for taking control of debt, spending, and planning for retirement. Overcome budget boredom by creating a vision and plan for the future of your finances. Don't just look at balancing the weekly or monthly budget as a dreaded task; look at it as an opportunity to demonstrate your faithfulness to God and your spouse as you responsibly plan for the future.

Quick Tip

The stress of your work duties, your role as a supportive spouse, your responsibilities as a parent, and all the other things of life can cause you to become overwhelmed. At some point you may just want to ignore responsibility and accept that whatever happens, happens. Don't allow apathy to rob you of the blessings good stewardship brings. This principle applies to many areas of life—not just to finances. Find a good time to talk about your finances, avoiding right before bed or anytime you are feeling exhausted. If that is the only time available, consider waking up earlier in the morning, grabbing some coffee, and talking about it over breakfast.

Sheepdog

You may feel it necessary to work ridiculous amounts of overtime just to make ends meet, and, while that is okay to an extent, it's unhealthy for you physically, mentally, and relationally to do so extensively. Let today be a challenge to get your finances in order, start a budget, and stick to it so you can work together to reduce the amount of overtime needed. Talk with your spouse about your finances, and if you don't have an established working budget, consider seeking out a resource to help you get started.

Spouse

Assuming your spouse is aware of an expense without direct communication can often lead to feelings of disrespect, and this will destroy intimacy in your relationship. While it may sound like a fundamental element of marriage, many couples report that they seldom, if ever, discuss finances. Talking about finances together is a great opportunity to enhance and improve communications and intimacy in your marriage. When was the last time you and your spouse discussed finances? Talk with your spouse about your dreams for the future together and how budgeting today can help you achieve those dreams.

Questions for Discussion

- What are the advantages of having a budget?
- How would a budget help your marriage right now?

Heavenly Father, before we can ask for more financial provision, we simply want to thank you for always providing for us. We are grateful to be depending on you—you are a generous and loving God! Give us wisdom as it relates to finances and intimacy. Amen.

Thoughts on Giving

Let giving flow from your heart, not from a sense of religious
duty. Let it spring up freely from the joy of giving—
all because God loves hilarious generosity!

2 CORINTHIANS 9:7 TPT

Clark and Christine faced extraordinary financial difficulties in
their marriage. After the medical bills exceeded $140,000 from
Christine's surgeries, Clark took on extra shifts at the station and
worked a part-time job to help keep their family finances on track.
It wasn't enough, but in the end, they discovered a valuable truth
about the faithfulness of God. Throughout the entire ordeal, which
spanned six years, Clark had given faithfully to his church and
missions. Even when he was unsure of how they would make their
payments, he gave his tithes.

"Clark, stop giving all that money away, and you'll be able to
stop working so much. We need you at home," Christine urged.

He insisted on remaining faithful in giving, and over time,
God honored Clark's obedience and generosity.

The greatest feeling you can share in life is celebrating victory
together amidst life's challenges. When you choose to agree on

giving, you are aligning your marriage and finances with the promises of God's Word that exalt generous giving, a pure heart, and wise stewardship. Today, discuss the topic of giving—whether it is your tithes, donating to a mission, or supporting some other charity you have in mind. You will never fail with a generous heart! It is extremely rewarding.

Quick Tip

The topic of giving in church can be a major issue for many congregants. This is largely due, in part, to the immoral and irresponsible behavior of others who have abused their positions in the past. The lesson to take away from this is to know what good soil looks like rather than to refrain from giving entirely. Withholding generosity robs you of the favor and blessings of God. Seek out reputable, transparent, responsible organizations to give to that show regular signs of life and growth. In addition, discussing your finances with your spouse shouldn't be a constant power struggle. Be generous internally with your finances, transparent with each other, and generous in giving. God's Word will never fail as it pertains to giving.

Sheepdog

Being involved with the finances means you are willing to have regular discussions about income and expenditures with your spouse. There are some couples who still keep separate bank accounts and lack any transparency. Some even live like roommates with separate lives under the same roof. That's not love! That is greed, and it will rob you of every good thing in life. If you and your spouse haven't had an open discussion about finances lately, a discussion about giving is the best place to start. Get your heart in line with God's Word as it relates to giving, and He will show you how to get the rest squared away.

Spouse

Couples have often assumed that the other spouse either didn't care or didn't want to be involved with the financial discussions and decisions. Never assume. Even if your spouse tells you they have no interest in discussing finances and want you to handle everything, still, for your own good and for the sake of your marriage, give regular updates. Ask questions of your spouse regarding giving, regular bills, and income. Do you believe giving can radically change your life if done with a generous, joyful, and pure heart?

Questions for Discussion

- How do you feel about giving away a portion of your monthly income?
- When have you seen good things happen because you have given to others?

Heavenly Father, today, we want to thank you for a generous heart to give in our marriage. We ask you to grant us a heart for missions and obedience as it relates to our finances, time, and talents. We know you will bless the seed we sow and the tithe we joyfully give faithfully. Amen.

Golden Years

Good planning and hard work lead to prosperity,
but hasty shortcuts lead to poverty.

PROVERBS 21:5 NLT

Ryan and Leigh married when they were in their early twenties, and Leigh gave birth to their first child three years later. For the next two decades, they raised three children, worked two jobs each, and saw each other mostly in passing. The day came when all three of their children had moved out, and they suddenly felt like two strangers living together. Everything they had done for most of their marriage revolved around their children, and they had completely neglected their relationship. It was a difficult time of transition.

"I'm not sure I would have married Ryan then if we knew each other like we do now," Leigh reminisced. "The fact is, we had stopped talking years earlier. I mean, we talked, but it was never as friends—it was as parents. I wish we would have done something differently."

The story of Ryan and Leigh has become all too common in marriages today. With the best of intentions, the focus becomes survival, taking care of children, and paying bills. Nurturing the marriage relationship becomes the lowest priority of day-to-day life. Couples learn to tolerate but not enjoy each other. This is, in part, due to a combined lack of vision and priority. Where are you going to be twenty years from today? Most people do not marry their best friend with a plan to fail, divorce, or be miserable. You are intentional about your walk with Christ, as evidenced by your reading this devotional. Why not also be intentional about planning for your future and doing the necessary work to nurture your marriage and ensure it remains a priority? If you want your golden years to be golden, you have to begin preparing for those years today.

Quick Tip

If you are within reach of retirement and haven't begun planning your life after duty, involve your spouse. If you are already in a situation similar to that of Ryan and Leigh, start from square one, get back to the basics, and pursue your spouse with a passion. It will take time, but if the love you share for each other runs deep and you are committed to each other, you can make your marriage last a lifetime. If you are in the early stages of marriage and parenting young children, you need to know that while you are to love those children, take care of them, and provide for them, your marriage relationship should not fall by the wayside. Make time together as husband and wife, not just as mommy and daddy.

Sheepdog

Regular planning, budgeting, and prudent financial decision-making now can lead to a prosperous and enjoyable retirement down the road. There are many who do not include their spouse in the retirement discussion, robbing themselves of a rich future together. Take the time to include your spouse in the planning process for your retirement years as you are never too young or too early in the process to begin planning. What is one thing you can do now to plan for a better future together after retirement?

Spouse

Planning for retirement isn't something you may discuss daily, weekly, or even monthly, but it should have some space in the vision of your marriage. Think about what type of lifestyle you both desire post-retirement, what things you would like to do, and begin planning now. Make sacrifices starting early in your career in order to enjoy life later. Working together in this process will be more fruitful than treating it like an issue for only one of you to address. What is one way you can contribute to the conversation of retirement planning and your golden years together?

Questions for Discussion

- Ideally, when would you like to retire?
- What kind of finances would you like to have in place for retirement?

Heavenly Father, thank you for the wisdom to plan early, to follow the instructions found in your Word, and to work together in this process. Help us make the right decisions that will pay rich dividends throughout our life and into the future, not just in the present. Amen.

Bedroom Boundaries

"I have the right to do anything," you say—but not everything is beneficial. "I have the right to do anything"—but I will not be mastered by anything.

1 CORINTHIANS 6:12

While this isn't a professional counseling session, it is necessary to dive into the topic of boundaries in the bedroom since sexual sins can often creep in if we are not armed with proper knowledge, conviction, and perspective. There are so many opinions on what is and isn't good for a Christian married couple to enjoy in the bedroom, but it all comes back to Scripture. Is it permissible according to Scripture? You should use a three-point rule when discussing bedroom boundaries: Does it meet the standards of Scripture? Does it violate either of your convictions? Does it bring physical, emotional, or mental harm? If it passes the test, it is ultimately your decision.

Your marriage should be full of love, and your memories and experiences as lovers should be pleasant, not embarrassing, painful, or shame-inducing. There is more freedom for sexual intimacy in the bedroom of two sold-out believers in Christ than any place in this world! The passion is hotter, the intimacy more intense, and there is no lingering condemnation or shame. The boundaries you establish in your bedroom should be mutually discussed, agreed upon, and respected. Never force your spouse to violate their convictions and conscience for your pleasure, as this will permanently damage your sexual intimacy. This world is powered by greed, selfishness, and lust. Don't allow these influences to corrupt your heart, and never cross the boundaries you've established in your bedroom.

Quick Tip

Some will suggest, when it comes to admiring the opposite sex, that you can "window shop" as long as you don't "buy." The lust for others outside of your spouse is poisonous, toxic, and destructive. It will ruin your sexual relationship with your spouse because it establishes unachievable standards. There's no better person to experience the freedom, satisfaction, pleasure, and blessing of sex with than your spouse. Choosing to step outside your marriage for sex or any other form of intimacy is like driving a dagger into the soul of your spouse. If it doesn't bother you to think of it this way, you have shut off your heart to the convicting power of the Holy Spirit, and your conscience has become lifeless. Don't flirt with the boundaries of healthy, holy sex, and don't dabble with temptation. Aggressively and relentlessly resist it.

Sheepdog

The standard to gauge your sexual desires will always be Scripture. If the Word of God is not deeply rooted in your heart, it will be difficult to discern the difference between righteous, holy sexual desire for your spouse and lustful desires that violate Scripture and damage your marriage. Express your desires to your spouse, but don't be forceful with your approach. Always operate within the boundaries established by Scripture.

Spouse

One of the biggest and oldest issues in marriage is the idea that the man wants sex all the time and the wife never wants to have sex. Instead of looking at marital sex through the lens of supply and demand, consider offering sexual fulfillment of your spouse's needs before they ask. If you are the one who is often pursued, try becoming the pursuer. It ultimately doesn't matter who pursues who in the bedroom, just don't let the passion die. Treat it as a gift, because it is! Nurture it, tend to it, and protect it.

Questions for Discussion

- What is something your spouse does in the bedroom that you enjoy?
- What is something you both can do to renew your desire for lovemaking as God intended?

Heavenly Father, thank you for teaching us right from wrong, good from evil, holy from unholy, and helping us to adhere to these boundaries in the bedroom. Remind us that it is a good thing to enjoy sex in marriage but to do so in a way that is honorable to you and to each other. Amen.

Don't Withhold a Good Thing

So don't continue to refuse your spouse those rights, except perhaps by mutual agreement for a specified time so that you can both be devoted to prayer. And then you should resume your physical pleasure so that the Adversary cannot take advantage of you because of the desires of your body.

1 CORINTHIANS 7:5 TPT

"Don't touch me, John. You know I am exhausted, the mortgage hasn't been paid in two months, and we have needs other than sex. Why can't you get a second job when you aren't on duty? I'm doing all I can!" Veronica exclaimed.

After fifteen years of marriage, John and Veronica had recently found themselves in a financial struggle after the overtime budget was drastically reduced. Veronica worked part-time at a dentist's office in town, but the income wasn't enough to fill the gap. The stress caused by financial challenges had affected their marriage in a severe way.

You may find yourself in a situation where you are going through the motions in the bedroom. It's physically satisfying to one or both but there's absolutely no intimacy. Intimacy goes beyond the physical act of sex. It's a bond and passion you cannot buy, conjure, or elicit. It's developed through relationship and affection consistently over a long period of time. If you've been negatively affected by the stresses of life, whether it's finances, health, careers, or some other area, you need to know that withholding sex from your spouse is a dangerous, painful thing to do. You are setting your spouse up for failure while he or she is already feeling isolated. No matter how bad things are right now in any area of your marriage, if you work together for each other, honor God, and seek His healing, you can find yourselves thriving and not just surviving.

Quick Tip

When was the last time God withheld any good thing from you because of your past—the past He has forgiven and forgotten? In the same way, be generous with your spouse. Intimacy depends on your willingness to let go of past pain and work toward a more abundant marriage. Don't allow anger, frustration, or grudges to rob you of the joy derived from the gift of true intimacy.

Sheepdog

The needs and desires of you and your spouse will not always be in sync. Seek out the needs and desires of your spouse and diligently try to meet those to the best of your ability. While you may have a higher desire for sexual intimacy, your spouse may have a desire or need for other forms of intimacy. Meeting your spouse's needs without making demands in return will clearly communicate to them that you are more concerned about their needs than you are with your own. As you wouldn't want your spouse to withhold meeting your desires, do not withhold any good thing from your spouse. Be generous in all you give, through whatever means satisfy his or her needs. Generous serving leads to intimacy.

Spouse

It is selfish to have the ability and resources to meet a need and yet refuse to meet that need in marriage. Perhaps it is not sex but some other area of need. Intimacy goes much deeper than sex and does not apply only to physical intimacy. Don't accept the lie that it is acceptable to use sex as a means of reward or punishment for your spouse's behavior and actions. Instead, sex is a gift to be freely exchanged and enjoyed in marriage. You will hear many others discuss the frequency of their sex life, but don't fall into the trap of comparing any part of your marriage with that of others. Focus on making yours the best it can be.

Questions for Discussion

- What is one need you can meet for your spouse today that he or she would appreciate?
- What is one way you can foster a more intimate marriage today?

Heavenly Father, thank you for the gift of sex in marriage. We ask you to help us unlearn all the lies of the enemy and ideas we've learned from the world about sex and find the true intimacy, power, and beauty of the gift of sex when it is approached through the truth of your Word. We trust your leading and blessing, and we will seek to be good stewards of this beautiful gift to each other. Amen.

Break Up Hard Soil

Your sex life will be blessed as you take joy and pleasure in the wife of your youth. Let her breasts be your satisfaction, and let her embrace intoxicate you at all times. Be continually delighted and ravished with her love.

PROVERBS 5:18-19 TPT

Time and stress are two things that threaten your marital sex life. If you aren't making time to be together, date, have fun, and be alone, you will grow apart. Add to that the stress life throws at you coupled with the stress you experience working as a first responder or member of the military, and you have a challenging sex life. Intimacy in the bedroom is enhanced when other areas of intimacy are thriving. Find out what your spouse enjoys outside the bedroom and spend time with them doing those activities. Perhaps you will go to a movie or play, take a random road trip, spend time at the range and shoot a few boxes of ammo, stay at a bed and breakfast, or study a book of the Bible together. Simply be spontaneous and love your spouse. Your sex life will be blessed when you reject the temptation of another and run into the arms of your spouse.

Remember the first time you were together as husband and wife? Your time alone was passionate and rewarding. Then along came the stresses of life, complete with a packed schedule, and your sex life likely went down the drain. Break up the hard soil in the area of physical intimacy in your marriage. Make time to be alone, to date, to be persistent and consistent. Don't rush. Take your time. Your sex life will be blessed if you are gentle, kind, loving, and generous outside the bedroom first.

Quick Tip

Be willing to start from the beginning all over again. Don't pretend to know everything about your spouse's likes and dislikes when it comes to sex. Talk about it. Ask questions. Rediscover your passions for each other, and know that God created sex to be enjoyed within the confines of marriage. Take your time. Don't be in a rush. If you make an effort and treat your spouse the right way, your sex life can be better than ever before. More importantly, you will have a more intimate relationship with your spouse. Discuss your sexual preferences with each other.

Sheepdog

Tunnel vision can be deadly on the streets, but it can also be costing you a deeper, more passionate and intimate relationship with your spouse. Focus on doing things that nurture your spouse and other areas of intimacy and affection, and the rest will come. If you haven't been doing these things, it's not too late. Do one thing today to nurture intimacy in your marriage.

Spouse

Acknowledge effort. No human being can achieve perfection consistently, but if either of you are putting forth the effort to have a more resilient, intimate, and thriving marriage, honor that effort. The honor you show your spouse's efforts can encourage continued effort!

Questions for Discussion

- What is something your spouse does outside of the bedroom that makes you interested in deeper intimacy?
- What is one way you can show honor to your spouse's efforts today?

Heavenly Father, thank you for the gift of sex and the blessings it brings within the relationship we have as a married couple. We ask you to show us the path to true, powerful, and lasting intimacy together. Show us the truth in your Word and dispel the lies about sex the enemy has planted in our lives. Help us walk in total freedom in you in this marriage, and fan the flames of true intimacy in our marriage today. Amen.

Affirming One Another

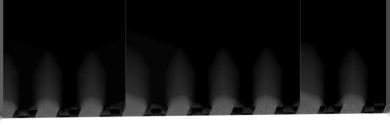

We Are Grateful for Each Other

Always give thanks to Father God for every person he brings into your life in the name of our Lord Jesus Christ.

EPHESIANS 5:20 TPT

It is too easy to take for granted what you have in life and find yourself riddled with envy, resentment, and discontent. But what if you vowed to live from a place of gratefulness, especially for your spouse and marriage? Gratefulness is the antidote to envy, resentment, and discontent. It tames the desire to always have more and leads to a heart that is content. Being grateful will create space for peace in your marriage, but it will also cause you to see the best in each other. Treating your spouse with gratefulness means you know your life would be lacking without them and the tremendous blessings they provide. You were created for each other and to help each other through this life—not just to survive, but to thrive.

If you've ever dealt with an ungrateful person, you know the poison ungratefulness produces. Lack of thanksgiving is toxic to anyone but can be disastrous to your marriage. When practiced daily, gratefulness can produce healthy benefits for a lasting and meaningful relationship. Count your blessings! Even in the midst of a fight, you can still be grateful. For example, someone who is ungrateful for their spouse will constantly desire more things, more changes, more stuff, and they will be flat-out rude and hateful when they encounter marital conflict. A grateful person will demonstrate loving compassion, display contentment, and approach conflict with love and grace. They will be a joy to be around!

Quick Tip

You were likely taught from a young age to be thankful for what you have in life. Your parents probably told you to "mind your manners" and say "thank you" and "please." The gratefulness you were taught as a child related to physical items, but as an adult you have learned that there is much to be grateful for in relationships as well. Create moments of gratitude with each other today. Living a grateful life isn't only good for your marriage, but it is also good for your physical and mental health. Decide together that today you will be grateful people who demonstrate thankfulness in all you do. Enjoy time together, do something kind, and find a way to inject gratefulness into your marriage today. You will find a life of gratitude produces an atmosphere of peace and harmony in which a beautiful marriage can thrive.

Sheepdog

Letting your spouse know you are grateful for them being in your life is a wonderful way to affirm him or her as your spouse. Demonstrating gratefulness on a regular basis creates an atmosphere for the miraculous and the abundant. Actions that say "I am grateful for you" will generate a beautiful exchange between you and your spouse.

Spouse

Everyone wants to be valued and appreciated—they want to know they are noticed and not overlooked in this world. In your marriage, you both make many sacrifices for each other, and those should be acknowledged in some way. Don't allow the attitude of "well, that's his or her job" to take precedence in your home. Such thinking fosters selfishness and is one of the number one killers of marriage.

Questions for Discussion

- Why are you grateful for your spouse?
- What is one way you can demonstrate today that you are grateful for your spouse?

Heavenly Father, we come to you today with a heart of gratefulness for who you are, for all you've done, and for blessing our marriage. Help us live and love in a way that is a constant demonstration of thankfulness and gratitude. Amen.

Give and Receive Love Freely with Each Other

Many waters cannot quench love; rivers cannot sweep it away. If one were to give all the wealth of one's house for love, it would be utterly scorned.

SONG OF SOLOMON 8:7

There is tremendous power in the expression of pure love. When you withhold love from your spouse through unforgiveness, resentment, or bitterness, you are essentially telling them they are not worthy of love. You are to be a vessel of God's love—receiving and expressing His love freely. Nothing can stop the love of God from reaching your life if you live with an open heart and receive what He has for you, but you must also live with open hands to give love away. Your spouse is more than deserving of the best love you can give—not what is left over at the end of the day.

Don't be satisfied with the state of your marriage—it's a way of letting your guard down and allowing the enemy to gain a foothold and sabotage it all. Your marriage deserves the best effort consistently—not just when it is easy. When you choose to be selfish, go to bed mad, or withhold forgiveness, you are not loving freely. Instead, you are withholding the best you could give your spouse. Think of God's love. It is impossible to conceive how he displays the depths of His love time after time, even when the world is so undeserving. How then can you ever resist loving anyone, much less your spouse? Give love freely to your spouse in every way possible. Never let circumstances squelch the love you have for each other.

Quick Tip

The fire of passion, intimacy, and unity in your marriage can be squelched out but the love God has for you never can. If you will obey His commands and love, honor, and respect each other in marriage the way He instructed, your love will not be easily diminished. It is possible to have a marriage that embodies the love described in today's verse, and this occurs when you are on fire for each other. Have life's bumps and bruises made you tough to love or reluctant to give love? Don't stop loving! It's up to you to keep the love flowing in your marriage like the mighty rivers of this world. Loving extravagantly means you give proper attention to your spouse, not neglecting your relationship. Neglecting your spouse will lead to divisiveness in your home and ultimately a void in your life.

Sheepdog

Instead of withholding any good thing from your spouse, find ways that express your love to them that will bless them. If you are upset or angry toward your spouse, that is the best time to step in and intentionally love them, not ignore or neglect them. Show your spouse love today in a way they will be absolutely blessed and blown away by. Overwhelm them with a display of love they will recognize and watch the walls between you crumble to the ground. Nothing can squelch the love God has for you, not even the worst and most abominable sin. To love your spouse as Christ loved the church, you shouldn't allow anything to come between you. Today, reaffirm to your spouse the unrelenting, unwavering, unsquelchable love you have for them.

Spouse

What joy and comfort it would bring to know that the love you share with your beloved spouse is impermeable and resistant to external forces! Your spouse needs to know there is nothing that will change your love for them, nothing that will shake your love for them, and that you are on their team.

Questions for Discussion

- What is your spouse's primary love language?
- How can you clearly communicate your love to your spouse today in a way that is most meaningful to him or her?

Heavenly Father, thank you for your unmovable love—a love that cannot be quenched. Help us love each other with the same kind of love you have demonstrated toward us—unrelenting, unconditional, and authentic. May our love for each other reflect you in our marriage. Amen.

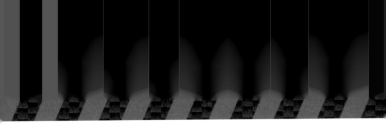

Forgive Each Other Easily

If you forgive anyone's sins, their sins are forgiven;
if you do not forgive them, they are not forgiven.

JOHN 20:23

His frail hands reached for the door. He was one of the last surviving World War II veterans, and I had been called to escort him to his doctor's appointment. We struck up a conversation, and I soon discovered he and his wife had been married for over fifty years. Knowing the value of this man's wisdom, I asked if he would be so kind as to share one important thing I could do to benefit my marriage.

With a weak and quivering voice, he replied, "Be quick to forgive. Never be too proud to say 'I'm sorry' first, even if you don't believe you are in the wrong. Kiss your wife each day and tell her at least once a day you love her. Have fun together. Dance together spontaneously. Life is short, and before you know it, you won't be able to take long walks together, so take those walks, hold her hand, and let her know you will never abandon her."

Allowing unforgiveness to build up in your heart creates severe issues in your marriage. Forgiving does not mean you will forget, and recalling a past offense doesn't mean you didn't forgive. It is imperative to remember this principle, because on more than one occasion, the offense will come to mind. It is what you do with the memory that determines if you have truly forgiven your spouse. Forgiveness defers judgment to God instead of claiming personal responsibility to hand down the judgment. It is not our place to bear the burdens of unforgiveness and resentment—the Father alone carries those burdens and has permanently relieved you of being the bearer of such things.

Quick Tip

If you were to be brutally honest with each other today, would there be any hidden unforgiveness in your marriage? The root of unforgiveness is selfishness, anger, and hatred. These things can lead to bitterness, unfruitfulness, stagnation, and powerlessness. It may seem that the offense you are still writhing over is insignificant to your spouse, but between you and God, that unforgiveness is creating a major block in your relationship. Be quick to forgive freely and let God handle the consequences. Start with a clean slate today. No matter the past, set the course for your future on an even path today. Today, express forgiveness of any of your spouse's offenses at any point in the past. It is not important at this stage for them to acknowledge any guilt. Just focus on offering forgiveness freely so bitterness can be eradicated from your marriage.

Sheepdog

Withholding forgiveness from your spouse creates contention and strife in your relationship. It is possible to forgive without forgetting, but forgiveness given freely is an act of faith and obedience to God's Word. No matter how bad it may seem, take a small step of faith and forgive whatever offenses your spouse has made against you. Today, examine your own heart and see if you are harboring any unforgiveness toward your spouse, and give those things to God in faith.

Spouse

To forgive is to stop being angry or resentful toward someone or to cancel a debt. Maybe your spouse has given you reason to be angry or resentful toward them, having sinned against God and causing you pain through their actions. If you withhold forgiveness, you are saying you have more insight and wisdom than God and that your spouse is not worthy of forgiveness. The Bible says you are forgiven only when you forgive. Your act of faith to forgive your spouse can be the start of a reconciliation process in your marriage. Today, ask your spouse if there are any unaddressed offenses that need forgiveness in your marriage, and then offer that forgiveness freely.

Questions for Discussion

- What offenses need to be addressed in your marriage?
- How can you make things right with your spouse?

Heavenly Father, thank you for your willingness to forgive us time and time again after we have sinned against you repeatedly. Thank you for your merciful refusal to give up on us. Today we come to you and seek your strength to forgive ourselves and each other of offenses, hurt, and sin, no matter how deep the pain. Even if we cannot see a way to forgive, we choose to follow your commands in faith. Give us the strength and courage to forgive, and we will do so in obedience to you. Amen.

Communicate Expectations Clearly

Timely advice is lovely, like golden apples in a silver basket.

PROVERBS 25:11 NLT

Growing up in a home with a close-knit family, Brianna found her expectations of marriage to be unlike that of her new husband. David and Brianna had been married for two years, and things weren't going how she'd planned or dreamed they would. He worked late hours and was seldom home in time for dinner, and she was becoming increasingly unhappy.

"David, we need to talk," she said one evening as they prepared for bed. "I never see you, and we've had only one meal together in the past two weeks. This isn't what I envisioned when I married you."

David didn't understand why he was being attacked. He considered the long hours he worked as an expression of his love and provision in their marriage. Both David and Brianna were in desperate need of help to resolve these issues.

Expectations never come without comparison. David hadn't realized how influential Brianna's upbringing was to her, and their expectations of each other in marriage were never communicated.

He had been raised in a home where his father was gone for work most of the time, and it was justified as his expression of love and investment in their family. Your marriage will never be better than your willingness to clearly communicate expectations and then take the necessary and appropriate actions to meet those expectations. If you want something from your spouse, or if you want something from your marriage, talk about it.

Quick Tip

When you set uncommunicated expectations, you are setting the stage for future resentment. It's easy to create resentment in your mind in response to something you've never even talked about—something your spouse probably has no clue is even an issue. Expectations communicated are "lovely, like golden apples," and the power of clear expectations lovingly expressed can cause you to actually desire to please your spouse. Clearly, concisely, and lovingly communicate your expectations. Don't demand anything of your spouse, but simply let them know your expectations regarding a major or minor issue. Maybe you've never had a discussion like this with your spouse before. You are robbing yourself of a great joy! Do not permit assumptions to be the guide to your marriage.

Sheepdog

If you have failed to communicate what you expect from your marriage—regardless of how insignificant it may seem—take time to talk about those things today. Maybe you've allowed assumptions to carry your marriage thus far, but without a solid vision, clearly communicated and well-executed, you will not have a bulletproof marriage.

Spouse

For many, simply communicating expectations in marriage can establish groundwork for emotional freedom. This can serve as a pivotal moment in your marriage, setting you free from the possibility of mutual resentment later and instead positioning you both for rich blessings.

Questions for Discussion

- What expectations do you have of your spouse?
- Where do you envision your marriage in the future?

Heavenly Father, thank you for opening our eyes to the power of clearly communicated expectations in our marriage. We know that as a couple committed to each other for life, we must have open and healthy communication. Never let us assume expectations are known if we haven't communicated them. Help us clearly communicate our expectations to each other today and in the future. Amen.

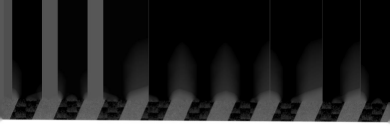

Conquer Challenges Together

If either of them falls down, one can help the other up.
But pity anyone who falls and has no one to help them up.

ECCLESIASTES 4:10

The smell of gunpowder was still fresh in the air. Unsure if the threat was eliminated, Jones looked over to his partner while trying to catch his breath and reload his service weapon.

"You take the A corner," Jones' partner directed. "Andy is bringing up the rear. I will cover you. I've got your back, brother. Let's get this done."

It was the first active shooter situation in which Jones had been involved. Despite all the politics found in law enforcement, and despite so many other insincere promises of "I've got your back," he had found two men who meant it with their entire being. You never know who is really by your side until you face the heat of conflict together. Times of peace reveal a person's dreams, but conflict unveils their character. Choose to remain committed to your marriage, your family, and keep your promises even when things are tough.

When the bullets start flying in your marriage, you have two options—quit and run away like a coward, or dig in your heels, load up, and cover each other. Attack the battlefield of life back-to-back, laying down suppression fire to make it to your next destination. It's almost like a dance, really. You move in sync while firing the arrows of God's Word to neutralize the attacks of the enemy and conquer the circumstances of life. There's no promise you will make it unscathed, unscarred, or unaffected, but you can make it through unconquered.

Quick Tip

Times of peace can be times of rest, but they should also be used to prepare for times of conflict and adversity. Don't grow complacent in your marriage if things are going perfectly right now. Make sure you are doing the necessary things to keep your relationship on the right track. Your motivation should be wisdom, prudence, and pure love rather than fear. Will you stay in the fight with your spouse when bullets start to fly, or will you run?

Sheepdog

No matter what the current state of your marriage, there's a seed of hope for improvement. You can contribute not only to the lifespan and health of your marriage but also invest in the life of your spouse. Don't become blindsided by the challenges of life and allow them to cause you to lose sight of the fact that your spouse is a child of God too. Today, reaffirm with your spouse that you are in this marriage for life, in peace and conflict, through any situation.

Spouse

Fear has a way of paralyzing you and causing you to refrain from taking any action. Hesitation can be deadly on the field of battle, but in your marriage, it can contribute to conflict. Never hesitate to grab the weapon of God's Word and do battle together with your spouse. Let them know they are never fighting alone, no matter how they feel. This will empower them and strengthen your marriage.

Questions for Discussion

- What is one way you can prepare for conflict together today?
- How do you want to show your spouse that you have his or her back in a crisis?

Heavenly Father, thank you for placing us in each other's lives so we wouldn't have to be alone. Thank you for giving us the courage to support each other in times of peace and conflict and for the heart to do battle against the enemy—to step in and provide the support we each need in difficult times. We acknowledge the goodness and blessings you have placed on our relationship and, without you, we have no hope for a bulletproof marriage. We choose to run to the fight together with you leading the way. Amen.

Respect Each Other

You, my brothers and sisters, were called to be free.
But do not use your freedom to indulge the flesh;
rather, serve one another humbly in love.

GALATIANS 5:13

Bill and Jenna began their relationship in high school nearly twenty years ago. During their dating years, Bill would get angry at Jenna for something she said or did and be verbally abusive. Jenna grew up without a father in her home and took the abuse as a normal part of any relationship. But she still struggled with how she was treated.

Five years into their marriage, Jenna and Bill attended marriage counseling where these issues were addressed. "I remember thinking in our first year of marriage, *I cannot imagine living like this the rest of my life. Someone who loves me isn't supposed to talk to me and treat me this way,*" Jenna recalled. She had been on the verge of walking away from her marriage to Bill for years but stuck it out. For this couple, counseling gave them the tools they needed to restore their marriage and give them both hope for the future.

Respect your spouse enough to talk with them about issues

you are dealing with. While respect is a pivotal element in any relationship, it is paramount to the success of your marriage. Both of you should desire to respect the other, not demand respect from your spouse. When you respect your spouse, you respect his or her emotions, feelings, thoughts, dreams, and input and will not be abusive in any fashion. Today your marriage may not be the best it can be—you may still have serious issues to address—but begin taking that step of faith in obedience and watch what God will do in your home!

Quick Tip

Submitting to your spouse doesn't mean they are better than you or have more rights than you. Submission is a demonstration of the love of Jesus to your spouse, the love that moved Him to give *everything* for the bride of Christ. Today, demonstrate to your spouse that you place a high value and worth on them and the value they bring to your relationship. If you can't see the value they bring to your marriage at this time, demonstrate that you value them for who they are and what they contribute as an act of faith.

Sheepdog

Demanding respect never produces results—it only creates more tension and conflict. Respect can be earned, but what if the respect you offered in your marriage brought about a mutual respect from your spouse? It's not enough to simply treat your spouse with respect; you must communicate with respect, and your spouse must receive what you are giving them.

Spouse

There are plenty of messages about the need to give and show respect toward your spouse, but few share how to recognize and receive respect. When your spouse treats you in a way that places your desires, needs, wants, feelings, and emotions before their own and at a higher level than other people would be treated, they are demonstrating respect. Submission and respect are two of the interchangeable, reciprocal, and needed elements in marriage.

Questions for Discussion

- What do you respect the most about your spouse?
- What is one area that you feel the need to mutually and humbly submit to one another?

Heavenly Father, thank you for teaching us how to respect each other and how to recognize respectful actions. We know our words are powerful, but they fall empty when our actions do not match the words we speak. Help our words of respect always be matched by our actions of respect. Amen.

Honor Each Other

Love is patient, love is kind. It does not envy, it does not boast,
it is not proud. It does not dishonor others, it is not self-
seeking, it is not easily angered, it keeps no record of wrongs.

1 CORINTHIANS 13:4–5

When Marcus was asked why he no longer wanted to remain married to his wife of seven years, he responded, "I don't feel like her heart is in the relationship any longer. It seems like we go through the motions, but there's no heart—something critical is missing."

In his comments, Marcus expressed a crucial aspect of honor—it originates from the heart. You can respect others' behaviors, actions, beliefs, and even differences, but honor originates from the heart.

Honor is the platinum edition of respect, and the purest form of love. Honoring your spouse means you don't treat them like they are replaceable or second-best, and you don't criticize them in public or behind their back; instead, honoring your spouse means you are endorsing them to the highest degree, with the highest esteem. The lack of honor in a home is a sure indicator of trouble to come. Where one or both spouses lack honor, they will abound in selfishness and disrespect. Maybe you've never experienced true honor or haven't been shown how to demonstrate honor toward another person. The good news is that it's never too late to dig into God's Word to see what He says about showing honor to your spouse.

Quick Tip

Honor your spouse by doing the things that leave a lasting influence on your marriage—worshiping together, serving God together, showing affection, listening, and communicating effectively. Your efforts and contributions are what lead to demonstrated honor in your marriage and richly protect and insulate your marriage from outside negative influence. Honor is the fuel and motivation for all the things you do for your spouse.

Sheepdog

To honor your spouse means you place him or her on a pedestal above the rest of the people in your life. You hold your spouse in the highest-esteem, and you are driven to love, cherish, and respect your spouse from a heart motivated by honor. It's not just a virtue meant for the professional life of a sheepdog—it is for your most intimate relationship with your spouse. You honor and respect those you serve side by side with. Do the same for your spouse. They aren't behind you, they are right next to you. You can honor your spouse today by giving the best you have to offer them, not reserving your best for someone else.

Spouse

Sometimes, demonstrating honor looks a lot like showing respect, but respect is most always tied to behavior and action. Your heart will always reveal the true motive, and if you don't have the right motivations, your actions will not last in tough times. When conflict comes, a person of dishonor will abort the relationship to satisfy their own needs, desires, and wants instead of fighting for the team.

Questions for Discussion

- What is one way you can honor each other while in public?
- How can you prioritize your marriage above other relationships in your life?

Heavenly Father, thank you for revealing the true meaning of honor to us. This revelation can radically change our marriage and the way we treat others in our lives. We ask you to show us the meaning, purpose, and way to honor you and each other every day. Amen.

Love Each Other through Challenges

And to the husbands, you are to demonstrate love for your
wives with the same tender devotion that Christ demonstrated
to us, his bride. For he died for us, sacrificing himself.

EPHESIANS 5:25 TPT

Throughout your life, there will be times when the *feeling* of love,
attraction, and intimacy fades and is replaced with routines, stress,
bills, and disagreements. This is a prime place to demonstrate
sacrificial love. There is no power in love if you only love when it is
convenient, easy, or beneficial—in fact, that is hardly love! A true
demonstration of love isn't found in the words you express; rather,
it is revealed when you are faced with difficulties, challenges, and
the need for forgiveness. Christ has demonstrated unchanging,
sacrificial love for the church, and today's verse lays down a hefty
challenge to demonstrate your love with tender devotion—the same
sacrificial love Christ has shown you repeatedly.

Marriage isn't always flowers, kisses, sweet words, and long
walks on the beach. There will be times you must choose to love
sacrificially through the hard stuff of life. Loving in this manner
first requires a full understanding and revelation of the love of
Jesus. To love as Christ loves the church means you must move

beyond your surface emotions and superficial words and move into the depths of what He has done for you! How can you refuse to love your spouse sacrificially when Christ has loved you so well? It is a sin to withhold such beauty from the one God has given you to spend your life with.

Quick Tip

Loving sacrificially is a virtue you must discover, develop, and demonstrate. You first discover it by understanding the power of God's love demonstrated in your life; you develop this love by practicing it daily; and you demonstrate this magnificent love by giving it when it is inconvenient or difficult to do so—even when it seems your spouse is unworthy and undeserving of such love. Sacrificial love may require you to give up something you enjoy for the sake of peace in your home. Resolve to demonstrate sacrificial love, regardless of what you think is deserved.

Sheepdog

Perhaps you have been deeply hurt by your spouse. Maybe you've discovered some painful, gut-wrenching secret that has blindsided you, and now you cannot see how to continue in your marriage. You have a clear option before you—you can choose to resent your spouse, withhold forgiveness, and become bitter, or you can choose to love sacrificially. The path will not be easy. That is why it is a "sacrificial" love—it is going to cost you something. It's going to require you to step outside your comfort zone. In challenging times, choose love.

Spouse

Love takes on many forms—you can love a song, movie, or pet, but none of these forms of love are sacrificial or even the same type of love you share with your spouse. You wouldn't sacrifice your life for the love of a song or movie, but you may be moved to make tremendous and costly sacrifices because of the deep love you have for your spouse. It is ultimately up to you and your spouse to define what sacrificial love in action looks like in your marriage. Christ has already demonstrated this love for you. How can you ever show such magnificent love for your spouse? Define sacrificial love as it relates to your marriage, and ask God to help you walk that out today.

Questions for Discussion

- In what way does your spouse demonstrate sacrificial love?
- When have you chosen to love in times of challenge?

Heavenly Father, we are overwhelmed by the revelation and power of your unconditional, unwavering, sacrificial love. It has changed our lives in so many good ways! Help us demonstrate the power of this love to each other every day we have together on this earth. Amen.

Appreciate the Actions of Your Spouse

The LORD God said, "It is not good for the man to be alone.
I will make a helper suitable for him."

GENESIS 2:18

In a study of 468 married couples conducted by the University of
Georgia in 2015, a secret ingredient—possibly the most critical
element to achieving a lasting relationship—was discovered:
gratitude. This often overlooked and underused method of
expressing a simple "thank you," was found to be a positive
disruptor of conflict, particularly when it came to stress and conflict
caused by financial issues.[3] True gratitude cannot be an expression
of mere words that lacks corresponding behavior. Grateful
hearts don't suffer from materialistic discontentment, and they
understand the reciprocal value of gratitude. You see, a person who
is ungrateful will take for granted the presence of another person,
including the things that person does. Soon enough, this ungrateful
heart becomes a clear and present danger.

Today, start approaching life with a thankful mind, thankful

---

3   "*The Power of Thank You: UGA Research Links Gratitude to Positive
Marital Outcomes*," EurekAlert!, October 21, 2015, https://www.eurekalert.
org/pub_releases/2015-10/uog-tpo102115.php.

thoughts, and a genuinely grateful heart rather than superficial, repetitive, empty affirmations of gratitude. You can show you are grateful for your spouse and all he or she does by helping them with duties at home, communicating meaningfully with them, and simply telling them you are thankful for all they do in your marriage. Sometimes, a simple "thank you" and a smile will go a long way. It's the daily habits of expressing gratitude that will make a profound difference in your marriage. Begin today by resolving to express appreciation and gratitude for each other.

Quick Tip

Sometimes, it's the little things we take for granted in our lives. If your spouse works hard, long hours, or if they prepare a meal for you, mow the lawn, or take on an extra project, let them know how much you appreciate what they do to contribute to your family. Don't assume they know you appreciate them—communicate it clearly and often. When you do, be specific and sincere. This can be one of the richest things you do in your marriage. Throughout the day today, express your appreciation for all the things your spouse does. Make a list of the good deeds!

Sheepdog

Comparison robs us of the joy gratitude gives. Don't allow this weed of life to choke out the beauty of the garden God has entrusted you to keep. The more you express gratitude for your spouse, the more grateful you will become, and the more you'll recognize the good qualities of your spouse. It's really all about perspective. You can see the sky as falling or see yourself as soaring closer to the clouds. Your spouse will have some bad qualities, but so do you and every other person who is, was, or will ever walk this earth. Put the actions of your spouse and their good qualities on a pedestal and express your gratitude for them.

Spouse

Your heart was created to remain full of love and gratitude. That's the original state God intended, but the fallen state of man has corrupted your heart, and now you depend on the presence of God to radically impact your life. Today, help your heart by expressing gratitude. It's one of those things that increases the more you give it, the more you see it, and the more you receive it.

Questions for Discussion

- What are ten qualities you appreciate about your spouse?
- What are ten things your spouse does that you appreciate?

Heavenly Father, thank you for showing us the proper way to approach you through the example of your Son, Jesus. Continue to show us the deep power of thankfulness and keep our hearts focused on the right motives. Help us honor you and each other with our thoughts, words, and deeds today. Amen.

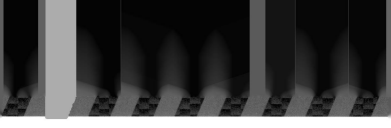

A Spirit-Led Marriage

But the Holy Spirit produces this kind of fruit in our lives:
love, joy, peace, patience, kindness, goodness, faithfulness,
gentleness, and self-control. There is no law against
these things!

GALATIANS 5:22–23 NLT

"Listen up!" bellowed the team leader, commanding everyone's attention. "We know the threat. We know the potential. But we have also spent countless hours preparing for a situation just like this. Remember your training. Do your job. Don't leave a man behind."

Shortly after the briefing, the first flashbang was thrown. A loud, thunderous blast hit the door, and their operation was underway. Just like they had trained, everything went as planned. No one was harmed, and the bad guys were taken to jail.

"Isn't it funny how training just works?" Jim and his partner, Norm, had conducted these operations hundreds of times.

"Well, Jim," Norm replied, "we've trained enough and done enough of these things, but still, I don't want to relax and pay the price."

Just like training produces various positive benefits in your service, the Holy Spirit produces gifts and fruit in your life. Training produces well-executed missions, safe troops, lower complaints, and less crime, but the Spirit produces love, joy, peace, patience, kindness, goodness, faithfulness, gentleness, and self-control. The law of your region controls what you can do with your training, but there is no law against the fruits of the Spirit in your life. These beautiful fruits will build thriving lives and magnificent marriages! But, just like training only helps those who let the knowledge become part of their person, the fruits of the Spirit only come when you invite the Holy Spirit into your life and allow Him to radically change you from the inside out.

Quick Tip

To produce the fruits of the Spirit, you must first be filled with the Spirit, know the Word, and walk in obedience with the Father. Your marriage will become exponentially sweeter when these fruits are produced! Spend time in the Word, ask God to fill you with His Spirit, and begin to sow the seed of these fruits in your marriage. Soon you will have a bountiful harvest to enjoy, with which you can honor God.

Sheepdog

Think about the fruits of the Spirit listed in today's verse. How much more enjoyable would your life and marriage be with all of these things present? You can believe the negative, toxic, poisonous words of this world, or you can walk in the fruits of the Spirit. One path will produce fear, death, and defeat while the other produces life, victory, and joy! It's your decision, and the first step is a step of faith in obedience to His Word.

Spouse

When Jesus said He came to give you abundant life in John 10:10, He meant more than financial abundance. While there's nothing wrong with financial abundance, it shouldn't be your primary focus. An abundance of the fruits of the Spirit would allow your marriage to flourish, and for that reason, you should seek out God and watch His Holy Spirit radically affect your life and marriage. Today, ask God to help your marriage become a bountiful harvest of the fruits of His Spirit.

Questions for Discussion

- What is the role of the Holy Spirit in your marriage?
- How would the presence of the fruits of the Spirit positively impact your marriage?

Heavenly Father, thank you for providing us with a Comforter—the Holy Spirit. Thank you for giving us a mind to seek you and the guidance to be good stewards of the gifts you have given us. As we seek you and become closer to you, we ask that you would cause the fruits of the Spirit to become visible and present in our lives. Amen.

Love Each Other Unconditionally

Our love for others is our grateful response
to the love God first demonstrated to us.

1 JOHN 4:19 TPT

It is impossible for you to claim to be a child of God if you don't extend love to those who love you, much less to those who you may perceive as unlovable. We are indebted to God because of the perfect, unconditional love He has extended to us. When you love others, you are demonstrating a grateful heart for the love God first showed you. You didn't invent it or create it, but you can be a good steward of it! When your spouse annoys you, gets on your nerves, and makes you angry, remember this love. You can say how much you love each other, but until it becomes part of your life as love in action, it only amounts to vain, empty promises.

Start your day today by declaring your love unconditionally for each other. Then show that love throughout the day. You can rest assured that this love will be challenged. It might be easy to come up with a list of excuses to end a marriage, but why not fight to keep your marriage together and thriving? Having unconditional love means behavior, circumstances, and feelings will never affect your relationship. Nothing. It is rock-solid, unwavering, permanent.

Will you be courageous enough today to declare this powerful love over your marriage?

Quick Tip

The enemy is going to throw everything he has at you to destroy your life, marriage, and family. You should see this challenge as an opportunity to throw everything in your life at the feet of Jesus and let Him guide your life. The love, grace, and freedom provided by Jesus' sacrifice doesn't grant us permission to sin. Rather, it sets you free from sin, shame, guilt, and condemnation. When you strive to love each other as Christ loves, it means you want to constantly demonstrate a grateful heart that seeks to give. Today, remove the ultimatums from your marriage. No more fine print, no more disclaimers—go all in. Trust God, trust each other, and watch God do His best!

Sheepdog

Don't let the evil and pain you see in this world cause your heart to become hardened, cold, and callused. The only antidote to this is to open up your heart to the life-changing love of God. He doesn't cause pain, evil, or sin—He is present with you through it all. This is a fallen world, and more than ever before, your spouse needs to know your love for them is unconditional, irrevocable, and unchanging. Behavior doesn't affect love.

Spouse

God is love, and His love is shown through the changed lives of those who have accepted His offer of unconditional love and redemption. This doesn't sound anything like religion does it? Religion often places stipulations on "love" but doesn't teach unconditional love—a powerful, earth-moving, life-changing love. This may require you to unlearn any previous definition of love.

Unconditional love is the only way the Father loves us, and we should love our spouse the same way.

Questions for Discussion

- How do you define unconditional love?
- How can you express unconditional love to your spouse today?

Heavenly Father, we ask you to overwhelm us with your love and help us do the same to each other as husband and wife. We cannot explain it well enough, nor can we adequately comprehend your love, but we can openly and fully surrender ourselves to receiving your love. Help us, in our finite existence, to demonstrate this unconditional love to each other as best as we can. Amen.

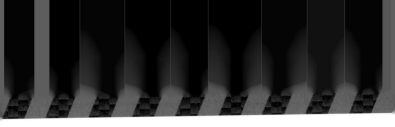

Secure with Each Other

No one has ever seen God; but if we love one another,
God lives in us and his love is made complete in us.

1 JOHN 4:12

Bulletproof vests provide protection from incoming rounds that would otherwise deliver a fatal wound. There are areas these vests cannot cover, thus, some areas will always be insecure and unprotected. This creates the need for cover in the event of incoming rounds. Wearing a bulletproof vest isn't comfortable and neither is wearing a concealed (or exposed) firearm, but these tools provide a degree of comfort in the knowledge of the protection that they offer. You can do all the right things in your relationship and have a bulletproof marriage all the way around, but there will still be certain areas that are vulnerable to attack. That's why you need the cover and protection of God and the help of your spouse.

Just like you are careful to protect vulnerable areas while wearing a bulletproof vest, you need to know what areas of your marriage are vulnerable and take action to safeguard them against attacks. This doesn't mean you are insecure in your marriage or that your marriage is weak; it is simply a reminder that no matter how much you grow in God or how far He takes you, there are still threats in this world. You should always be discerning but never insecure or living in fear of punishment. That's not the result of love but the result of evil and abusive behavior. You can nurture your marriage today by demonstrating a powerful, unconditional love for your spouse that produces peace, life, and power rather than fear. Remember, love doesn't produce fear, and any relationship where fear is used as a motivator to "get love" is a dysfunctional and abusive relationship.

How can you cover the vulnerable spots of your marriage?

Quick Tip

The only perfect security you have as an individual or married couple is found in an authentic daily relationship with God. There's no other protection available. Choose the perfect love of Christ as the model for love in your marriage. You are loved so well and perfectly by God—even in your mess. He calls you to love your spouse with the same passion and abandonment.

Sheepdog

Every day presents a new opportunity to demonstrate a perfect love to your spouse. Everyone has a different story, and maybe your spouse dealt with fear as a motivator to force them to give love as a child, or some other abusive situation. The Father can use you to demonstrate a pure love in daily living, to show what His love looks like on this earth. You don't have to wait until you get to heaven to experience perfect love; you can practice it daily. Eliminate fear and insecurity from your marriage by walking in the power of the Holy Spirit, and watch what God does in your marriage!

Spouse

Talk with your spouse about any insecurities either of you have about your marriage relationship. Are they justified? Or are they lies of the enemy? Know that love doesn't produce fear, and fear is a liar. Sometimes you will discover these thoughts and feelings are attacks by the enemy that can be eliminated through a simple conversation with your spouse and fervent prayer. If you have any feelings of fear and insecurity in your marriage, talk with your spouse today.

Questions for Discussion

- What is something your spouse does that makes you feel secure?
- How can you cover the vulnerable parts of your marriage as it grows stronger?

Heavenly Father, today we rest in the peace, security, and safety we know you provide. This world is not our home, and we know the dangers are real. However, we choose to believe you have a higher purpose for our lives and marriage. Help our lives demonstrate that your love produces peace and not fear, and help us love each other with this same love. Amen.

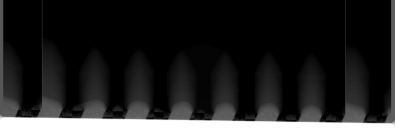

Grow More Attracted to Each Other

You have captured my heart, my treasure, my bride.
You hold it hostage with one glance of your eyes,
with a single jewel of your necklace.

SONG OF SOLOMON 4:9 NLT

Not every marriage is a nightmare, and not every marriage is a fairy tale—some are smack dab in the middle, just stuck in a rut of mediocrity. If you asked those couples in the middle, they'd tell you everything was okay and there were no complaints. They would also come up short in the compliments department. They wouldn't rave about how excited they are to see their spouse or spend time with them. There's a difference between serving out of obligation and serving out of love. Love-motivated service creates intimacy, develops favor, and leads to prosperity. This is how you can grow more attracted to each other every day you are together. Service that's motivated by love is a relationship game changer.

To avoid becoming a marital statistic, be sure you express your affection to your spouse, but also let him or her know how much you are attracted to them. It doesn't have to be a complicated compliment. You can start by complimenting them from the head down or the feet up, or you can start complimenting from the inside of who they are to their outward appearance. No matter what, take a few seconds every day to admire your spouse's beauty and tell them you are attracted to them. Tell them what you find beautiful, not just "you are beautiful." Specific compliments are far more memorable after the moment has passed. The only way to grow more attracted to each other every day is to open your eyes to the complete person your spouse is—their soul, their heart. Outward looks will change, but the heart remains a true beauty to behold.

Quick Tip

If you want to open the eyes of your spouse, begin by letting them know you have eyes only for them. If you are always breaking your neck to compliment someone else but ignore your spouse, you are robbing your marriage of a passionate connection. Attraction between spouses can be nurtured by meaningful expression. While the outward appearance is certainly eye-catching, look deeper. Go beyond the surface and watch the facial expressions, attitude, and approach your spouse takes to marriage change in a very positive manner.

Sheepdog

Attention is a powerful, intimate form of expressing attraction. Who are you giving your attention to? Break the mundane routine in marriage today. Add another bulletproof layer by letting your spouse know specifically what "soul" attraction you have. Maybe it is their faith, their unwavering love and support, or some other element of their inner person. Go beyond the surface. You may have trouble expressing yourself with words, but don't let that stop you. Willingness to be vulnerable in this manner can radically change your marriage for the better. If you aren't going to tell your spouse all the ways you are attracted to him or her daily, who will? They need to hear it from you often and directly.

Spouse

Every person is "wired" differently with different gifts and skills, but you can always find a way to share loving words with the person you are attracted to. Some may not like describing first responders and military members as warriors, but that "label" is certainly embraced when they are needed in times of conflict. Tell your sheepdog what attracts you to them. Don't let this act cause you to be embarrassed or feel inferior or inadequate. If you are completely uncomfortable vocalizing your attractions, write them down instead. It doesn't have to be complicated, but this can be a premium expression of love, affection, and intimacy for your spouse.

Questions for Discussion

- What inner qualities of your spouse are the most attractive?
- What external traits of your spouse do you find the most attractive?

Heavenly Father, today we thank you for the soul ties that bind us as husband and wife and for the attraction we have to each other. Help us never lose sight of the soul attractions, and always keep us aware of the physical attractions we have for each other. Today we declare that we grow more attracted to each other through your power and love each day. Amen.

Express Your Feelings to Each Other

Nothing is more appealing than speaking beautiful,
life-giving words. For they release sweetness to our souls
and inner healing to our spirits.

PROVERBS 16:24 TPT

Rick took the time to write out the last letter his wife would read
if he were killed in the line of duty. As he wrote it, something
happened in his heart. He had never spoken the words he had just
written to his wife.

"In all the years I have loved Mary," Rick confided, "I never
expressed to her the things I was writing in my letter. I began to
think, why would I want to keep these feelings and thoughts from
her until I am gone?"

What a rich revelation he received in a challenging moment! It
often takes men and women their entire lives—until their deathbed
moment—to understand what Rick discovered through writing
his last letter. He realized that the feelings, thoughts, and emotions
he wanted to convey posthumously could radically change his
marriage in the present and have a profound impact on his wife.
He took the next opportunity to share his letter with Mary.

And if you are reading this, it means I didn't finish well. It means I didn't make it home. It means I gave it all for you, and you need to know just how much I love you. For all the times we fought—for every time I made you cry—I am sorry. But I want you to remember me for the times we celebrated and loved.

Tears began to run down both their faces as Rick expressed his deepest feelings for his beloved wife. Don't wait until you are at death's door to tell your spouse how you feel. Don't wait until tragedy strikes to tell them how much you love them. The riches of this life are found in the moments we choose to be vulnerable and express our deepest, most sincere and heartfelt emotions to our spouse. Will you be vulnerable today?

Quick Tip

If you are unsure where to begin expressing yourself to your spouse, begin at the end. Write down the things you'd want to say if you had thirty minutes left to live. This isn't morbid; it's brave. This will break up any hard-heartedness and establish a new level of openness and authentic communication in your marriage. In all circumstances, be willing to be vulnerable with your spouse. Your marriage is a safe space, a place you can express your deepest feelings.

Sheepdog

Of all the people in this world, you know the frailty of life. Never allow pride, ego, or hardness of heart to keep you from the richness found in transparency. This isn't a sign of weakness, fellow sheepdog; this is a sign of tremendous strength and courage. Your marriage will bear much fruit from these moments! They should not be rare moments, but rather, moments every day! Don't let a moment go by without letting your spouse know how deeply you love them, how passionately you care for them, how wildly affectionate you feel about them. Shake off those dry bones and speak fresh life into your marriage today.

Spouse

Think of a single moment when you were both vulnerable with each other in a very real way. Do you remember it? One of the greatest regrets most couples have is that they shared their feelings for each other too late in life and not frequently enough. You can change that today. At the end of the day, you only leave this world with what you give away. Give the best of yourself to your spouse every day. Cherish your time together. Celebrate each other's successes and comfort each other in difficulty.

Questions for Discussion

- What is one thing you would say to your spouse right now if this was your last minute alive?
- What is one thing you want your spouse to remember about you forever?

Heavenly Father, thank you for the gift of perspective, for the courage to be vulnerable with each other, and for the heart to trust you with it all. Teach us to number our days and to love each other as you love us—unbridled. Amen.

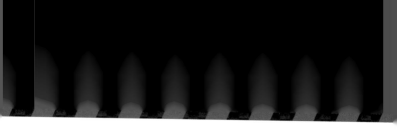

Continue to Do Life Together

Two are better than one,
because they have a good return for their labor.

ECCLESIASTES 4:9

"What are you doing!?" The gruff voice of the sergeant pierced the ears of his subordinates.

"Sir, finishing the assignment you gave me," Jackson said.

"You'll never finish if you choose to do this alone. What about Roberts? Are you going to let him finish by himself? I guess you are a one-man operation, is that what this is? Are you trying to prove something?"

Whether he wanted to admit it or not, Jackson had been taught a life lesson in a moment of conflict with his sergeant—a lesson of teamwork, camaraderie, and not relying on your own strength alone. Too often, the focus can be on getting the job done, not doing it together or doing it as one. Toxic tunnel vision can take over, making it easy to lose sight of the strengths of the entire team. This is a fatal mistake in marriage.

There are many times when you can accomplish more with the help of another. Manual labor is certainly one of those things, but as a sheepdog, you often count on backup to come assist with difficult situations on the job. It would be a difficult task to do this life alone, without any companionship, friendship, help, or backup. Even from the very beginning of existence, when God created Adam, He knew it wouldn't be good for him to be alone. How compassionate, supremely wise, and caring of God to create a companion for him! Sure, there are times when both of you want to be alone—many people want time to themselves. But imagine having no communication with anyone every day and doing everything by yourself; it would get old and lonely quick. Marriage provides the blessing of companionship so you can complete the labor of life side by side with the one you love!

Quick Tip

Two are better than one when the two involved are willing to put forth a genuine effort to improve the marriage, but two can be devastating if one or both have quit trying! This is heartbreaking, sad, and all too common. Stop walking through life like a numb zombie—no emotion, no feelings, no passion—just working, sleeping, eating, and waiting to die. That is no way to live and is certainly void of any joy. The words in this devotional are countercultural and will be considered obsolete and outdated by so many, but your marriage will shine like a beacon in the night! You have been exposed to the Son of God, and He will bind you and your spouse together for His glory.

Sheepdog

Don't let your spouse work all day, all week, and then come home and prepare your meals, clean your clothes, feed the kids, and chase the pets, all while you enjoy a game or show on TV. Sharing duties around the home is such a small portion of doing life together but so important to keeping in sync with each other. We should love each other enough to see when our spouse is exhausted, show compassion, and not want them to do more than they have to do. If you see your spouse trying to tough out a task alone, reach in, show initiative, and try to help.

Spouse

Make room for your spouse to help and don't criticize if they do try to help, especially if the help they offer isn't the way you do it or up to your standards. If you were to insist on serving your spouse, you would have the best marriage you could dream of because love prefers others over self. Don't refuse the help of your spouse if they try to pitch in, especially if this hasn't been part of your marriage culture in the past. Working together as a couple often means one tries to help and the other accepts the help. Allow your spouse to help you in life. If not, it's a sure sign of the presence of pride.

Questions for Discussion

- What is one thing you can do today to improve the bond you have as a couple?
- What is something you can do together that you normally do alone?

Heavenly Father, thank you for the gift of two. Thank you for the gift of companionship, help, and someone to enjoy life with. Help us see the blessing and value in each other's life, gifts, and heart. Guide our steps as we continue to live this life together for your glory. Amen.

SECTION SIX

Oneness

Aligned Affections

In this same way, husbands ought to love their wives
as their own bodies. He who loves his wife loves himself.

EPHESIANS 5:28

Marriage was created to reflect the love Christ has for the church,
but this is not possible when selfishness is prevalent. Jesus loves
sacrificially and unconditionally—not just when you live right
and please Him. Your goal should be to love your spouse with an
unconditional, sacrificial love as Jesus loves the church. The opposite
of sacrificial love is a selfish person who does not truly know love.
As followers of Christ, you have His nature living in you, and He
is love. You cannot truly love until you first know the love of God.
When you allow the Word of God to take root in your heart and
embrace the true power of who God is—allowing Him to change
you from the inside out—then you are able to love like Christ.

At some point, you will no longer "feel" in love, and there
may come a time when you no longer feel like showing affection
to your spouse. In the same way, if you work out in the gym a lot,
there will be days you don't "feel" like working out and you may
not always feel like you are in good physical condition—but you
are! Feelings and emotions can be deceptive, but your commitment

242

and profession of love for your spouse requires you to contribute and be an active part of the relationship. Showing affection and loving well are just the basics. Your relationship may be in shambles right now, but if you will put forth the maximum effort, combined with unwavering faith and consistent prayer, you will watch those feelings change to genuine, heartfelt action backed by sincere and pure motives.

Quick Tip

If your heart is set on the things of heaven and in pursuit of a relationship with Jesus daily, your affections will be demonstrated in the same manner. Keep in mind that affection is not something that's just expressed in material gifts, physical intimacy, or things that require an investment of emotions or time. The key is the amount of effort and love placed into showing affection. You know Jesus loved you all the way to the cross, and He still loves you. Together as a married couple, define what tangible, demonstrated love looks like to you.

Sheepdog

Find ways to show your love for your spouse. Not everyone shows or receives affection the same way. You know your spouse and you know what he or she likes. Find one sure way you can demonstrate your love for your spouse today and do it! Set your affections on things above, not on the temporal things of this world. When you both pursue the affections of heaven, together you will have aligned affections and experience a deeper unity.

Spouse

Are your affections communicated *and* demonstrated? You can say how much you love your spouse, but do your actions match your words? Find ways to express your affection for your spouse in ways they will notice, understand, and appreciate. Don't wait for them to be the first to take initiative and show affection to you. Be the one to take the first step.

Questions for Discussion

- How do you like to give affection?
- How do you like to receive affection?

Heavenly Father, help us love each other in a way that reflects your unconditional, unrelenting love for your church. May our words be covered with grace and love as we seek to honor you in all we do in life. Amen.

Peacekeepers at Home

In peace I will lie down and sleep,
for you alone, LORD, make me dwell in safety.

PSALM 4:8

For many years, Steve and Lauren handled marital conflict by yelling at each other, ignoring each other, and then completely shutting off communication.

"I'd rather have peace and quiet; the only way to do that is just let it go," Lauren shared with a friend after a recent disagreement.

The argument was never resolved. Instead they let it go, sweeping it under the rug and pretending it no longer existed. On the surface, things looked okay, but years of unaddressed issues were speeding this formerly blissful couple to a destructive end.

"My biggest problem, I guess, is that I want Lauren to listen to me," Steve confided in a friend. "I want her to hear me out, but she never lets me finish my point. She always interrupts me, and we eventually end up yelling over each other's voices."

It was clear neither wanted to continue the conflict, but they had no direction for finding and keeping peace in their marriage.

Ephesians 4:2-3 lays out a path for peace in marriage—through humility, patience, gentleness, and generous love. Marital harmony is found when you love each other with a fervent, Christlike love—a love with no strings attached that favors your spouse over yourself. It's not an easy assignment, but it is a necessary one. If it isn't in your heart to make things right in your marriage, if it isn't in your heart to keep trying, it's time to check your heart and implore God to help you model it after His own.

Quick Tip

To achieve peace, you must first know the Source of peace and be willing to follow His lead through conflict and adversity. The quality of your marriage relationship will depend on your mutual willingness to navigate through challenges using the truths found in God's Word. Addressing conflict in the wrong way—striving to do everything on your own—can be destructive to your marriage relationship. Together, rest in the peace of God's promises and protection today.

Sheepdog

Take some time to look inward. What occupies your heart? Are you full of love for God and your spouse? Are you willing to continue working toward a harmonious and fruitful marriage? Demonstrate humility toward your spouse by prioritizing peace over winning an argument. Demonstrate patience with your spouse. Show love, be gentle, and strive for oneness in your marriage. Division between two people who love each other is a painful thing. Spend time today cherishing your spouse.

Spouse

If there has been a history of strife and contention in your marriage, the fastest way to find peace and begin down a path of healing and harmony is to forgive. Forgive with no strings attached. Even if your spouse becomes agitated or upset, remain at peace with them. Don't allow their disgruntled attitude to extinguish your peace. Also be sure to pray for the Spirit of God to invade your home, your marriage, your heart, and your spouse. Miracles are not outdated, and God can do mighty things through fervent prayer. If you will commit to praying for your spouse and your marriage daily, peace will become a present help and the key to overcoming the conflict in your lives.

Questions for Discussion

- What prayers have you seen answered in your past?
- What do you want your spouse to pray about for you today?

Heavenly Father, thank you for the calling to establish peace in our world. We ask you to give us the knowledge and self-will to keep peace in our marriage through our words and actions. Amen.

Quick Draw

Make allowance for each other's faults,
and forgive anyone who offends you.
Remember, the Lord forgave you,
so you must forgive others.

COLOSSIANS 3:13 NLT

"Would you shut up? I am so sick of hearing about your problems! All you had to do was pay the bill on time like I told you to."

James didn't waste any time letting his wife, Sarah, know how he felt about the electric being disconnected at home.

"James, please. It was an honest mistake," Sarah stammered.

Between chauffeuring their four kids from home to school and then ball practice, dealing with two sick kids, and her part-time job, Sarah had her hands full. For two weeks, James reminded his wife of five years about her mistake, but it became more a serious issue when he began attacking her personally.

"Are you losing your mind? I mean, you have nothing else to do, how could you forget to pay one bill?" His incredulous words echoed through the house.

Had James been willing to walk into their home and wrap his arms around his wife and say, "It's okay honey, it was just a mistake. We can work through it," this story would have had a much happier ending.

The journey of life is one filled with learning moments, growth opportunities, and plenty of chances to demonstrate the love and grace of Christ to others—especially to your spouse. You are bound to make a mistake in your marriage at some point, and you probably have already made a few. Be quick to forgive your spouse, and do not be easily offended. You have no right to withhold forgiveness, no matter how deep the pain, since you are not the Author of forgiveness. You are merely called to be a faithful steward of the forgiveness you've freely received.

Quick Tip

To be the best, professional athletes strive for perfection. This demand for perfection often comes with a high price tag that includes stress, burnout, and resentment. Neither you nor your spouse will be perfect, but don't let that be an excuse to abandon the pursuit of perfection and excellence in your marriage. Instead, acknowledge a reasonable margin of error, give grace freely, and don't be so quick to issue judgment or criticism regarding your spouse's failures.

Sheepdog

When you set an expectation in your mind of how you believe your spouse should act, you have already established a standard in your mind about how they should live. The reality is, this standard will always be unreachable for your spouse and anyone else you measure against it. This type of thinking also positions you to expect perfection and face the shortcomings of your spouse with resentment and criticism. Don't expect yourself or your spouse to be perfect; freely offer as much grace, margin, and forgiveness as you would like at your very worst!

Spouse

Making room for each other's faults doesn't mean you are condoning wrong behavior—it means you are demonstrating understanding that your spouse is human, and you see the mistakes you have made too. A rigid set of rules will lead you to become disappointed, frustrated, and ready to throw in the towel. Instead, give yourself and your spouse room to make mistakes. There will be times when you both have a bad day, but it doesn't mean you are having a bad marriage. Forgive as often as you desire forgiveness, and demonstrate grace freely in your marriage.

Questions for Discussion

- Why is it difficult to forgive sometimes?
- How have you seen another's forgiveness bring positive changes in your life?

Heavenly Father, when we come to you seeking forgiveness, you are always quick to forgive and never remind us of our sin again. We ask you to help us forgive each other more quickly than we judge or criticize, as you have never held back forgiveness from us. Amen.

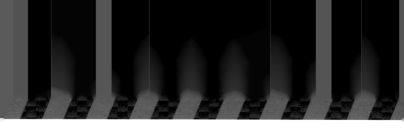

Have Fun Together

A cheerful heart is good medicine,
but a crushed spirit dries up the bones.

PROVERBS 17:22

As they pulled into the parking lot of the theme park, Ronnie quickly reminded his wife he would not be riding any roller coasters.

"Aw, babe, come on. It'll be fun" she exclaimed.

"For you it will. Not for me." He went on to make his case why he would not be participating in any of the rides, and his wife's attitude immediately changed.

"All we do is work, Ron," she pleaded. "We work all the time and never have any fun, and I want to do this together. Please, I want to have a great day with you! I have been looking forward to this!"

They made their way into the park, grabbed their tickets, and off they went. A few hours passed, and before he knew it, Ronnie was having the time of his life. They laughed, ate more than they should have, and ended the day with dinner and passionate lovemaking. Maybe roller coasters aren't such a bad thing after all!

One secret to marriage longevity that veteran couples swear by is choosing to invest in laughter and fun. They enjoy each other. Life is short, sometimes stressful, but it is always improved with genuine laughter. Having fun is great preventative medicine for your marriage! Take time away from the daily hustle and mundane work to enjoy each other's company. There's no reason to take life so seriously to the point that you no longer laugh or enjoy being married. Have fun, enjoy your spouse, and laugh together. It's good for your marriage, it's good for your health, and it is great for your sex life.

Quick Tip

You will find adventure outside of your comfort zone. There are things that may cause you to be afraid, and that's okay. Ride the roller coasters, see a movie, enjoy your time together. Do something exciting—something you've never done before. Go bungee jumping, skydiving, horseback riding, or take a cruise together. Break away from the monotony of life and inject some adventure, laughter, and fun into your marriage. Plan and schedule a surprise date with your spouse. For the fullest enjoyment, be sure to keep your plans a surprise.

Sheepdog

It's easy to become cynical, hard-hearted, and callused with all the things you deal with daily, but rise above the threshold of a negative environment and be the salt and light described in God's Word. Find something you like doing together in your marriage— something fun and adventurous—and explore the possibilities found through enjoying your spouse! Don't let your marriage grow stale as you age; maturity doesn't mean boring! Take your spouse on a camping trip, go on a hike, go fishing or hunting together, go to concerts together—do something other than work and pay bills! It may be an event you aren't a huge fan of, but catering to your spouse's needs and desires will pay rich dividends!

Spouse

Choosing to live a life of adventure may mean you have to take a step outside your comfort zone or even do things you aren't accustomed to doing. Try something different—find something you both enjoy and do it together. If multibillion-dollar corporations spend millions on team building, don't you think your marriage should focus on this area too? After all, you're trying to create unity and oneness in marriage, not competition or division.

Questions for Discussion

- What do each of you like to do for fun?
- What is your best memory of fun together as a couple?

Heavenly Father, thank you for the gift of laughter and joy. When life seems to be overwhelming, remind us to laugh and have fun. Never let us take for granted the joy of our marriage. Amen.

Grow as Friends

His mouth is sweetness itself; he is altogether lovely.
This is my beloved, this is my friend, daughters of Jerusalem.

SONG OF SOLOMON 5:16

The first time they met, his heart raced. His hands began to sweat, his face turned beet red, and he stumbled over his words. Instead of love at first sight, it was nerves at first sight.

"I, I was wondering, would you like to go to dinner sometime this week?" He managed to stammer weakly. Chris was never the most popular guy in the office, often seeming like a loner, but he had mustered up the courage to ask Dana out.

"I'd love to!" she exclaimed. "I'm free Thursday, how does that sound?"

"Great, I will pick you up at seven. Is that good?" He knew he would replay her answer in his mind for the next few hours, willing Thursday to arrive more quickly.

The rest is history. They went to concerts together, talked about the future, work, and eventually began talking about marriage. That was over twenty years ago. Today, Chris and Dana have been married for nearly eighteen years and never stopped dating each other. Maybe it sounds like a fantasy to you, but they placed a priority on protecting their friendship and keeping the passion alive.

It's not easy staying friends in marriage through difficult times, and that's why the vow to remain committed is vital. Commitment is for the hard times. Anyone can stick out the good times. Remember the passion you had when you first began dating? You couldn't get enough time together. What changed? Priorities, stress, bills, children, and time all played a role in the numbing of your friendship. It's time to reawaken that friendship. It will require work, effort, and consistency, but it is not impossible. Before you were lovers, you were friends, and before you were parents, you were lovers. It's time to revive the passion of your youth. Take your spouse on a weekly date, be spontaneous, break up the routine in the bedroom, have fun. Make time for each other. Sit and talk about things that interest your spouse, limiting your discussions about finances or children to times outside date night. Plan your future together. Plan a trip. Take a vacation without anyone else, just the two of you.

Quick Tip

Friends don't seek to harm each other. In fact, true friends are more interested in each other than they are in themselves. Selfishness will destroy your life and marriage, leading you to certain demise. While it may seem you are too busy to work on your marriage, friends make time for each other—they never sacrifice their relationship for something of lesser value. This is true wisdom. Before you were lovers, you were best friends. It's time to enjoy your friendship as husband and wife and abandon the old, unfruitful mind-set of a dead relationship after marriage.

Sheepdog

If you were to attempt to start a friendship by talking about yourself all the time, you would find it very difficult to have any friends. It would be impossible! Selfishness inhibits relational development. But, if you express genuine interest in the other person's life—who they are and what they love—you will find they will express the same for you! This basic relationship principle has fallen by the wayside in marriage. Express more interest in your spouse than you do in talking about yourself. Selflessness will lead to a rich and fruitful marriage.

Spouse

The mystery of marriage is that you both have unique stories, characteristics, personalities, and differences, but you still long for each other. Your past may not be a beautiful one in your own eyes, but it has prepared you for these moments. Will you choose to express interest in the things your spouse loves, enjoys, and appreciates? Doing this ~~consistently over time~~ will lead to a bull~~etproof~~ marriage because it will foster trust and intimacy.

Questions for Discussion

- What is one thing you would like to learn about your spouse today?
- What is one thing you would like your spouse to learn about you?

Heavenly Father, thank you for my best friend—my spouse. Thank you for healing any hurt that may exist in our marriage and reminding us that you don't remind us of our mistakes. We ask you to help us grow closer to you as a couple, and to grow closer together as friends and lovers. Amen.

Day 81

Defend the House

As the Scriptures say, "A man leaves his father and mother and is joined to his wife, and the two are united into one."

EPHESIANS 5:31 NLT

After announcing their engagement, Alex and Julie soon found that not everyone celebrated their upcoming union.

"I give it six months at best," said Julie's mom.

This alienated Alex and created a conflict between the newly engaged lovers. In a critical moment, Julie's response established a boundary that would serve as a driving force for her new role as wife to Alex.

"Mother, that is not your place. Alex and I have been dating for more than eighteen months and have prayed about this. We even talked to you and Dad about it. Alex is going to be my husband, and that is the end of it. This is not your decision. Please respect our decision and our relationship."

Maybe you've found yourself in a similar situation as Alex and Julie with your parents or in-laws. Whatever the case, do not allow anyone to create a wedge between you and your spouse. Establish solid boundaries and stick to them. Support your spouse, not your

257

parent. Your relationship with your parents is important, but if you are not actively defending your marriage and your spouse, you will soon find yourself alienated and experiencing division in your relationship. Addressing parents and in-laws should still be done with tact, love, honor, and grace, but know it is necessary to be firm and consistent. At the end of the day, no matter what, support your spouse and your marriage.

Quick Tip

Your parents, friends, or other family may try to interject their opinions into your marriage for any number of reasons. The fact is, the only authority to make decisions in your marriage lies with you and your spouse. This isn't a suggestion to isolate yourselves from family and friends; just be careful when allowing others to speak into your lives. Don't talk negatively about your spouse to your parents or your in-laws. This doesn't have to be a sour relationship, and in fact, it can be a blessed one when there are clearly communicated expectations and boundaries. Defend your marriage, protect your spouse, respect the in-laws.

Sheepdog

The threats to your marriage are real and they are many. This isn't the first time you've been outnumbered and faced victory. In fact, God's people all throughout His Word show how small numbers, with His help, can lead to tremendous victories. No matter the form of the threat, it's an attack of the enemy. The moment you took the hand of your spouse and promised "till death us do part," you promised to leave yesterday in the past and move into the future together. Don't try to do this on your own. Lean on the direction and wisdom of the Father.

Spouse

Allowing unauthorized outside voices to influence your marriage without your spouse's knowledge or blessing will lead to division in your home. It can erode the relationship of trust you have if those conversations are kept secret from your spouse—not to mention creating hurt and strife. Consider your spouse and the integrity of your marriage before confiding your marriage problems in *any* outside ear. If you are both aware and present during the conversation, and both of you are okay with the subject matter, that's different; but don't do these things without your spouse's knowledge. Protect your home by protecting your level of intimacy with others. Don't give an ear to the whispering seducer. Focus instead on God's truth in His Word and ask for His guidance in discerning how to approach this sensitive issue.

Questions for Discussion

- What strengths does your spouse have that make your marriage stronger?
- What is something you can do to protect your marriage more closely?

Heavenly Father, thank you for the blessing of our marriage, parents, and family. We thank you for helping us address with grace any issues involving our parents. Help us establish clear boundaries in our marriage and defend our relationship with love and respect. Amen.

Create a Vision Together

When there is no clear prophetic vision, people quickly wander astray. But when you follow the revelation of the word, heaven's bliss fills your soul.

PROVERBS 29:18 TPT

Never have the threats to your marriage and family come so often, so relentlessly, and from so many angles. You do not have time to be passive about your marriage or to wander aimlessly through life without a vision for your future. When was the last time you went on a long-distance road trip without a set destination in mind? You naturally plan and envision your destination and then enter the address into your smartphone or GPS and follow the directions. You know where you are going! Without a vision, you lack a destination. In marriage, you don't have to have your whole plan of life figured out—you just need to know where you are going, what you are fighting for, and then fight together to get it done.

Creating a vision together means you sit and discuss the different aspects of your life with your spouse. For instance, are children in the future? How do you want to parent? If you want to retire at a certain age, how will you manage your finances to reach that goal, and what sacrifices will be necessary right now to make it happen? How do you respond to adversity? Talk through your dreams and ambitions and set up a vision for where you want your marriage to be in six months, one year, five years, and even twenty years. Establish ways to measure the growth and strength of your relationship and do the work to make it happen. Plans are only as good as the effort and efficiency with which they are executed.

Quick Tip

If you have a common goal and common interests you are working toward with your spouse, it will keep you focused on the future as opposed to fighting for reasons to quit. It also keeps you from looking in the rearview mirror at your past. If you cannot imagine your marriage thriving, or if you cannot imagine growing old with your spouse, there's a problem. It can be resolved, but it is going to take getting back to the basics, being diligent and relentless in doing the right things, and a mutual commitment to each other. Imagine your best life together following the path God has set for you.

Sheepdog

As a sheepdog, you are familiar with strategy, planning, and creating a course of action. Have a conversation with your spouse about where you want to be in your marriage in three months, six months, a year, five years, and even twenty years and beyond. This may sound foolish, but it is instilling some core fundamentals that will bring you closer together. Once you establish a clear vision and plan, start taking the necessary steps. Leave Post-It Notes throughout your home and car that speak life into your marriage, declaring your joint vision as you take the first steps together.

Spouse

If the things you've done in the past haven't led to a fruitful and thriving marriage, it's time to change the things you are doing. The revelation of God's Word for your marriage means there's a hope and a future; you are destined for success if you both are willing, commit to do the work, and honor the heart of God. It's easy to walk away from something you can't imagine being committed to for life. Start today by spending time speaking life into your marriage—even if it is already in tip-top shape. Declare a vision and future over your marriage and spouse, then take action as God directs.

Questions for Discussion

- What is a common goal you are both working on right now?
- What is the next best step you both can take toward accomplishing that goal?

Heavenly Father, we are thankful for the marriage you have blessed us with. Today we ask you to give us a vision for this marriage. Show us the picture of what you created our marriage to be—not what the world says or what we may perceive—but what you intend for us. Direct our paths and we will walk according to your guidance. Amen.

Growing in Faith Together

Now faith is confidence in what we hope for
and assurance about what we do not see.

HEBREWS 11:1

There may be times when you can't see how your marriage will
ever work because of your circumstances in the natural realm. It
is in these moments when your faith requires action, because faith
without works is dead—that is, stale, no life, no power, no function,
no use. But, when you take action based on your profession of
faith, that active faith can have a massive positive impact on the
world. Your marriage is dependent on the presence of a living,
thriving, growing faith. This is the only way to please God—with
an active faith! In order to achieve this, you may need to reposition
your heart in such a way that you are totally dependent on God to
increase your faith in your marriage.

Growing together in faith means you are taking faith-based,
faith-powered action on a regular basis together. You cannot grow
in faith if you aren't taking steps outside your comfort zone. Your
faith certainly will not increase if you fail to be obedient to God in
every way. You can read the Bible, but if it is not applied to your
heart and life, its power will remain undiscovered. You know about

263

faith, but if it is not put to work, it is useless. You could be in the fight of your life and have all the tools to resolve the fight, but if you don't use them, they won't do you any good. Faith is a beautiful tool given by God for you to connect with Him, walk in the gifts of the Spirit, and live a Spirit-filled and empowered life. No wonder the enemy keeps planting seeds of doubt in your mind; he knows that if you two grab hands and grow in faith, you can radically change your world!

Quick Tip

Growing in faith together means you grow in faith individually and as a couple. You are going to the same heights and depths together. Faith is deepened through the thorough and right study of and obedience to God's Word and the leading of the Holy Spirit. From finances to fitness, parenting to politics, putting your faith to work will rock your world. Use it in every area freely, liberally, and without apprehension. Faith is the power that helps you soar!

Sheepdog

Be encouraged today if challenges are present. It is a prime opportunity to break out your faith and put it to work! Did He promise peace that surpasses all understanding? Lean on Him for that peace! Did He promise to meet all your needs? Lean on Him for that provision! Did He promise to strengthen you? Lean on Him for that strength. All the while, your spouse may be leaning on you for strength. Throw your burdens at the feet of Jesus, and He will empower you to live victoriously today.

Spouse

Some may say faith is a personal thing. Some may refer to faith as a body of religious organizations or religion in itself. Faith is an invisible power that puts the believer of Christ in a whole new playing field of life. When you put your faith to work, people will look at your life and wonder what is different. When your marriage is growing in faith, you will become a beacon of hope for those who desperately need the love of Jesus in their life. The power of active, living, dynamic faith cannot be underestimated. It will take you places you never dreamed. How can you activate your faith today? Speak His Word over your marriage.

Questions for Discussion

- In what situation do you want to see God move?
- What is one small way you can step out in faith together?

Heavenly Father, thank you for the gift and measure of faith in our marriage. Thank you for showing us the path to ever-increasing faith and what it means to put our faith in you to work! Help us never become stagnant and help us be good stewards of our faith in you. Amen.

The Freedom of Selflessness

Abandon every display of selfishness.
Possess a greater concern for what matters to others
instead of your own interests.

PHILIPPIANS 2:4 TPT

"Dan, how will we ever make this marriage work if you continue to spend hundreds of dollars on stuff for yourself when we are struggling to pay bills? I don't want to nag you, but we need to work on our communication in this marriage," Brianne confronted her husband of three years.

Initially they'd agreed no purchase of $100 or more would occur without mutual agreement or, at minimum, a discussion about the purchase.

"Brianne, I earn the bulk of our income. If I want to spend a couple hundred on stuff I enjoy, what's the big deal? I can earn more. I don't see what the issue is."

Dan was blind to his own selfishness. Some may agree with Dan that, since he was the "breadwinner," he could do as he pleased. He had bought the lie, and the poison of selfishness was destroying his marriage. The entire time he couldn't see it.

There's nothing wrong with treating yourself, but when treating yourself causes conflict or takes away from others in your home, it's a problem. Don't be selfish! Your interests are important, and it is okay for you to focus on them from time to time, but when a greater priority is placed on your interests than your spouse's interests, you are set up for destruction. Unity in your marriage is only attainable when both of you are selfless. In fact, some couples who have been married for over fifty years will tell you that selflessness played a role in their lives together. You can choose to be selfish, but you are sacrificing the power of a bulletproof marriage.

Quick Tip

Selfish love is putting your own interests ahead of your spouse's in a way that sacrifices the welfare of your spouse. Selfless love is sacrificial love, perfectly executed as a demonstration of the purest form of devotion known to mankind. Selfish love is a toxic, destructive way to live and will ruin your relationship with your spouse. Let all you do be an effort to love your spouse well, and if you cannot love perfectly, at least love selflessly.

Sheepdog

It is better to be more concerned with the needs and desires of your spouse than it is to be concerned with your own interests. In a world that is "me" focused, don't fall for the trap. It will end with you being lonely, unfulfilled, and destroyed. You can demonstrate selflessness to your spouse today by letting them know they mean more to you than you having your own way. Their satisfaction, peace, and comfort is more important than your temporary pleasure and satisfaction.

Spouse

Think about the love Jesus has demonstrated toward you. All He ever asked for in return was for you to accept His love and sacrifice. Selfless love is the best way to exemplify His love in action in your life. When you refuse to forgive, you are being selfish. When you choose to shut down and not communicate with your spouse to avoid conflict, you are being selfish. Choose the selfless path to a more unified marriage relationship today.

Questions for Discussion

- What is the most selfless thing your spouse has done for you?
- What is one area where you can demonstrate selflessness in your marriage today?

Heavenly Father, thank you for giving us the example of what total selfless love looks like. Help us to love each other as you have loved us and help us rid our lives of selfishness. Amen.

Unrestrained Love for Your Spouse

"The LORD your God is with you, the Mighty Warrior who saves. He will take great delight in you; in his love he will no longer rebuke you, but will rejoice over you with singing."

ZEPHANIAH 3:17

With the alarming statistics of porn addiction in America, it's obvious the nation has a flawed perception of love, attraction, and sex. Millions have been blinded to the true love of God and bought the lies that have nothing to do with His unfailing, steadfast, open arms of love. Fatherless children grow up having, in many cases, a skewed view of God's love and His nature as heavenly Father. They understand love with conditions or expectations, but God's love is so incredibly powerful, that it cannot be described in its fullness without experiencing it personally. Relationships in life would take a rapid turn in the right direction if believers and unbelievers had a clear perspective of the Lord God Almighty.

When you choose to seek love in places other than Christ or your spouse, you restrict your ability to give the best love, or even love at all. It distorts your view and knowledge of true love. Unrestrained love for your spouse means you've decided to no longer share those benefits with anyone other than your spouse. Ever.

Unrestrained love for your spouse is wild, free, and careless love. Have you ever wondered why people would dare question the power of love in marriage but embrace hatred with celebration? How can you attempt to love if you aren't going to do it well, according to the standard established in the Bible? God celebrates and delights over you when you return to Him, so you should at least smile when you experience reconciliation in your marriage. Don't get sucked into the traps of negative speaking and thinking, apathy, and cynicism. There's nothing good about those things. There's no doubt you will never be able to love like Jesus loved, but you can at least give it a solid effort. Give each other unrestrained love.

Quick Tip

Radical love is the type of love that causes you to give up things you enjoy with friends in order to be with your spouse. Sounds crazy, right? This isn't a love that is deployed in small amounts toward the heart of your spouse; this is a hard-hitting, massive deployment of love. A tactical form of love in your sheepdog marriage. This is an all-out, shock-and-awe love. Just when your spouse thinks there's no love or forgiveness left, overwhelm them with a demonstration of the Father's heart with wild love. Demonstrate this powerful form of love to your spouse today.

Sheepdog

Shock and awe. That's the level of love you are being challenged to show your spouse, at some point, in some way, today. Prepare a meal, or, as a special treat, surprise your spouse with dinner out. Do a household chore that isn't typically your responsibility. Be happy when you should, by circumstances, be beat down. If he or she is rude, be kind and loving. Whatever level of love you've established as "normal," blow the lid off and take it up three notches. Do it with no strings attached, no ultimatum, no desire or expectation of anything in return. Give love freely and often. Then watch your marriage get rocked by the power of God.

Spouse

Every time your spouse puts on a uniform to serve, they are demonstrating unrestrained, wild and free love for the community they serve. It isn't always met with celebration or thankfulness. You may be taken aback by your spouse's new demonstration of love for you, but welcome it with open arms and then find a way to reciprocate. Your marriage will never be the same.

Questions for Discussion

- What is the most extravagant expression of love you've ever experienced?
- How can you demonstrate unrestrained love toward your spouse today?

Heavenly Father, thank you for demonstrating your unrestrained, world-changing love for us. We are truly thankful. Help us demonstrate unrestrained love to each other in our marriage, and may all our steps, thoughts, words, and deeds honor you. Amen.

Abandon the Past

Let me be clear, the Anointed One has set us free—
not partially, but completely and wonderfully free!
We must always cherish this truth and stubbornly refuse
to go back into the bondage of our past.

GALATIANS 5:1 TPT

Trying to set sail in your life as a married couple while holding onto your past is like trying to launch a ship tied to the dock. It's impossible and often hurts innocent bystanders. Your marriage will only be as solid as the distance you place between where you are and the past that is behind you. The past has offered vital lessons to learn from, and you've grown from the experiences you've been through, but today, abandon the past once and for all. Leave it where it belongs—behind you. Resolve today that, no matter what, neither of you will ever revisit the bondage of your past.

Today, cut the anchors that have held you back from the best marriage possible. Cut the ties that have bound you to the pain of yesterday and set sail into the destiny God has ordained for your marriage. You have not been partially set free. Scripture says you have been completely and wonderfully set free! It is up to you whether you want to stay tethered in the past or if you will steer your marriage toward your destiny. There will certainly be raging storms, but your marriage was built to sustain, endure, thrive, and cut through the raging, thunderous waves of life. This is no time for timid prayers and reluctant actions of obedience. Pursue the Father and the destiny He has for you with passion.

Quick Tip

Dig deep to remove the roots of yesterday's pain and misery. Eliminate the negative by filling your mind and heart with the positive, uplifting news of God's Word. His healing is not some mythical occurrence; it is a real, tangible healing. His freedom isn't partial—it is total! Abandon the past mistakes and behaviors that created heartache and walk in the total freedom God has provided through His Son, Jesus.

Sheepdog

The farther you walk together into tomorrow, the more distant yesterday's bondage of sin will be. It's not easy, but it is well worth the intentional and consistent effort. Determine in your heart that you will persevere as one body for one purpose, and remember that if God has forgiven you and set you free, you are diluting the power of His love in your life by continuing to remember your past sins. Together declare yesterday off-limits and look at the vision God has created for your marriage. Agree with your spouse to forget the painful memories of yesterday and begin replacing those voids with the Word of God and the new memories He gives!

Spouse

You've heard the old phrase "You can lead a horse to water, but you can't make him drink." The same goes for the freedom provided by Jesus. He has cut the chains of bondage, but you may still be sitting there with the remnants of those broken chains on your body. You've been set free, friend. Get up and go with your spouse after the beautiful life God has created for you! This is a new day, a new life, and a new opportunity to honor the Father daily.

Questions for Discussion

- What past memories do you feel you need to let go of as you move toward a better marriage?
- What is a Bible verse you can declare over the area in which you most desire freedom?

Heavenly Father, thank you for setting us free! Now we walk in the power of new life with the promise of eternal life with you! Help us enjoy and walk in the freedom you have given us today and every day, ridding our lives of yesterday's struggles and looking for your hand in everything we do. Amen.

One Team

That all of them may be one, Father, just as you are in me and I am in you. May they also be in us so that the world may believe that you have sent me.

JOHN 17:21

"Every one of you will give me fifty push-ups for every minute the last runner takes to finish the run. You better help him finish or you will all be pushing up the world until breakfast tomorrow morning!" The training sergeant seemed intent on breaking the entire unit down before moving forward.

That day, fifteen recruits finished the run, but as a result of the slowest man finishing late, they all were forced to perform over eight hundred push-ups, in addition to the regular training and punishments that were issued. Before their twelve-week journey was finished, the group operated as a well-oiled machine. The weakest link soon became a driving force of motivation for the rest of the class and they finished well—together.

Marriage also requires the burden of hardship to be shared. The strongest must help the weakest link pick up the slack for the good of the entire team. Becoming one team means enduring pain

275

and joy together. It means the team bears the brunt of consequences for one person's actions, and the entire team celebrates the victories of one person. It's all for the good of the team. Today, shift your focus from a "what's in it for me" mentality to a "what's best for the marriage" mentality. Every action you take, every decision made, should be for the good of the team, not focused on what is best for one person, but for your marriage as a whole. If one suffers, both suffer. If one celebrates, both celebrate. If one is sick, both are in it together until a positive resolution develops. How can you create a "one team" mind-set in your marriage today?

Quick Tip

Be sure those who are speaking into your ear (and the ear of your spouse) are on your team, cheering for your marriage. This doesn't have to do with paranoia. It's just wise to be strategic with who you open up your heart and marriage to. Not everyone who embraces you will look out for your best interests or the best interests of your marriage. Be discerning. Make sure there is no one trying to sabotage what God is doing in your marriage. Aggressively protect your marriage against the enemies who would try to slip in through the cracks.

Sheepdog

You are familiar with the power of unity and the dangers of division. Nothing can create turmoil as fast and as deadly as selfishness. A selfless sheepdog is a heroic icon who can radically change his or her world for the better. You can change the culture of your marriage today with one daily act of selflessness, and a "one team" mind-set. Write down three benefits of having a unified marriage.

Spouse

There will be times you don't feel like one team. Conflict—whether it originates inside or outside the marriage—can cause you to feel like divided, opposing forces. Don't listen to the lies preying on your emotions. Instead, work more diligently to nurture and protect unity by communicating with your spouse. Demonstrate to your spouse that you are on their team and working to help their life and your marriage become richer and more fruitful.

Questions for Discussion

- What tactic does the enemy use to disrupt you from being a unified team?
- What two or three actions clearly demonstrate to your spouse that you're on the same team?

Heavenly Father, thank you for the beauty of becoming one. We ask you to help us recognize the little foxes that would create division and contention in our marriage. Show us the clear path to developing a "one team" mentality. It's all for your glory. Amen.

Day 88

No Plan to Fail

I have told you these things, so that in me you may have peace. In this world you will have trouble. But take heart! I have overcome the world.

JOHN 16:33

In their book *Extreme Ownership*, authors Jocko Willink and Leif Babin share extreme leadership principles that can be applied to any area of business and life. In one section, Willink and Babin talk about the fundamental of SEAL training—teamwork. There is no focus on the individual; it is all about the team. The core strength of any Navy SEAL unit is teamwork and unity. The loners are weeded out early in the process because each operator depends on the others to accomplish the mission. This depth of teamwork should be a pillar in your marital covenant. You depend on each other daily in marriage and nothing should cause division.

Create a pact today that you are going to be 100 percent committed to each other as one team, one body, one unit moving through this life together with one mission. There is absolutely nothing that will come between you. Your mission is clear. Your purpose is clear. You have what you need to successfully navigate the challenges and successes of this life—failure is not an option.

Marriage requires both of you to give 100 percent. If you're not willing to do that, it's time for a gut check. If you won't give 100 percent now, with this marriage, you are never going to give it all for anyone else in life. Today is a new day, and this is a new beginning. Go win together.

Quick Tip

Maybe you say you don't plan for your marriage to fail or you don't plan on having an affair. However, unless you take the proper action to prevent those scenarios from happening, you are fooling yourself. The reality is, many people have endured divorce and other trying relationship issues, and they will tell you they never planned for it; it just happened. If there's no plan to succeed as a couple, that in itself is a plan to fail. Set safeguards and be tenacious about protecting the unity of your marriage. Work diligently to have a plan for adversity.

Sheepdog

The moment you find yourself between the wolf and the sheep, you have no plan to fail. But if you have no plan, you are planning to fail. Perhaps you don't often think of marriage as needing a plan for success, but it desperately needs your leadership and planning skills. You do not train to fail, nor do you intend to fail. It's not part of the preparation process or language in your field of work. But too often, duty is where the "no plan to fail" ends. At home, if your marriage isn't taken just as seriously as your work-related duties, it will be more susceptible to failure. Do the work, have a plan, and lead your family by serving them well.

Spouse

You may say, "Things just aren't working out." That is no way to address a lifelong relationship commitment. Quitters are always going to be last and always starting over. Bulletproof marriages don't happen overnight. Having a solid plan to navigate your days together, as one team, whether you face great conflict or tremendous success, is crucial to the lifespan and quality of your marriage. Your plan may be something as simple as "we agree not to go to bed angry." It doesn't have to be complicated to be effective. Do you have a marriage success plan or a marriage fail plan?

Questions for Discussion

- In what areas have you seen success in your marriage?
- What areas in your marriage need a plan to succeed?

Heavenly Father, thank you for demonstrating order and strategy for us through your actions found in your Word. Today we ask you to help us create an effective plan to address and navigate life. Amen.

Let's Come Together

"But 'God made them male and female' from the beginning of creation. 'This explains why a man leaves his father and mother and is joined to his wife, and the two are united into one.' Since they are no longer two but one, let no one split apart what God has joined together."

MARK 10:6-9 NLT

Lewis walked up the sidewalk to his home and dropped his dark green bag full of gear. He'd been gone for almost an entire year, and his heart began to race as his wife and kids ran to greet him. The raw emotion of being reunited with his family was overwhelming, in a good way. His two children wrapped their arms around his neck simultaneously and squeezed their daddy tightly.

"We missed you so much, Daddy!" the youngest exclaimed.

As Lewis stood up, his wife, Mary Anne, covered her mouth with her hands, tears running down her face, then opened her arms to embrace her husband.

"You look so thin, babe." She held him tightly and moved her face back to look at Lewis. "I am so glad you are home."

When you look back on the original state of humanity before

281

the fall in the garden of Eden, you see the way your marriage was intended to be lived out. Not in misery or temporary relationships, but sanctified, permanent, and enjoyable. You were created to be fruitful, but the seed of Adam was tarnished in the garden, and Jesus was the only reconciliation that could restore you to a right relationship with God. Because of His sacrifice, no matter the distance separating you from your spouse, oneness remains. Remove the temptation to be selfish and give your spouse the very best part of your life. Work together to enjoy life the way God designed. You are never too far from each other and never too far from God to experience this overwhelming, satisfying, fulfilling unity and love. Work to protect the unity and togetherness of your marriage and family.

Quick Tip

There was a time when people meant what they said. There were no mind games or tricks. When someone said "I do," they meant it for life. Times have changed, marking a steady decline of morality in our society. Most of us would rather justify our sin because of our "rights" instead of living a life that is honorable and pleasing to God. There will be things and people who try to pull you apart for various evil reasons, but do not let them! You are a team—two people who, regardless of how you feel now, once expressed love toward each other.

Sheepdog

When duty calls you away from your family, it is often accompanied by a tug-of-war of emotions. You know your call to duty, but you also want to be with your spouse and family. The work you are called to do is noble and for a worthy cause, and the distance between you and your spouse is only temporary. Whether you are in your home together daily or separated by assignment, strive to always nurture the unity you share. This is the blessing of marriage and the great Creator's intended design.

Spouse

Coming together as husband and wife may mean you have to let go of some old negative feelings and reject embracing past mistakes as ammo for present or future arguments. It is also sure to generate some euphoric emotions derived from unity as well. This is because God crafted marriage to bond two individuals into one unit. While the process of becoming one isn't always easy, its fruits are bountiful and good.

Questions for Discussion

- What is one practical way to protect the unity in your marriage?
- In what areas do you want to grow closer in your marriage?

Heavenly Father, thank you for uniting us together as one body—husband and wife—and for helping keep our union of marriage as one after your heart. Amen.

Enjoy and Thrive Together

A thief has only one thing in mind—he wants to steal,
slaughter, and destroy. But I have come to give you
everything in abundance, more than you expect—
life in its fullness until you overflow!

JOHN 10:10 TPT

It may seem most days that your newsfeed is filled with stories of
horrible violence, rampant evil, and heartbreaking stories of tragic
loss. This is indicative of a world full of people who have embraced
darkness and serve the enemy, but it is also a reminder of the
many broken and hurting people in this world. This life will surely
present many troubles, but Jesus said to not be troubled because
He overcame the world. This promise applies specifically to your
marriage. If you can see the plot of the enemy before you, engage
in battle, and you will immediately know how to foil his schemes.
God wants you to be able to enjoy your spouse and live victoriously.

One of the subtle schemes of the enemy is to use the conflicts
and challenges of daily life to create division and animosity in your
marriage. It's a scheme he uses in minds, marriages, and families
to create turmoil. Now that you know this, you can be more aware
of these threats as they arise. To enjoy and thrive together in your

marriage, know that God's plan and desire for you is a life that is abundant in everything good! Being able to distinguish the difference between the plans of the enemy and the plans God has for you means you must know God through His Word—in truth and in Spirit. The only way to enjoy life and thrive together is to walk in a covenant relationship with the living Son of God—the perfect sacrifice offered for your freedom.

Quick Tip

We know the enemy has one thing in mind—to destroy you and make your life miserable, to rob you of the goodness and life God has for you. What are your intentions? Will you aggressively oppose the plans of the enemy to protect and nourish your marriage? This is the moment of truth for you. This is the place where the line is drawn in the sand. There's no cavalry coming to save you, God has empowered you to get this job done, done well, and done in victory. Leave nothing in reserve! Leave it all on the field of battle. If you want to experience the abundant life promised by Christ, you will have to fight for it. Not in works or deeds, but battle against the enemy and the thief who wants to take what you have. This is most effective in powerful prayer, declaring God's Word over your lives, and keeping your thoughts in alignment with His Word.

Sheepdog

The enemy is a liar, thief, and accuser. He wants nothing more than to destroy you in every way possible. The things that do not honor or glorify God, or that don't demonstrate a life changed by the love of God, are sin. You may be reminded often of the mistakes you made in the past, and you may even feel unworthy of God's love and forgiveness. These are lies of the enemy, meant to destroy your life and destroy your marriage. Fight the battles of life with your spouse as one body, one unit, and one team, just as God has designed.

Spouse

To thrive, you may have to cut some of the dead limbs—worry, anxiety, fear, and distrust—from your marriage. Focus on the basic building blocks of making your relationship with your spouse as fruitful and healthy as possible by eliminating negative thoughts and behaviors and applying the Word of God to your daily living.

Questions for Discussion

- What is a phrase you can use as a signal to each other that you want the best for your spouse and marriage?
- What would an "abundant" life together look like?

Heavenly Father, thank you for the gift of eternal life, for empowering us to be victorious in this life, and for coming to give us life to the fullest while we are here. Amen.

About the Authors

Adam Davis

Life for law enforcement officers is about as stressful as it can get these days. They're constantly on guard—weighing whether the person approaching is friend or foe. Is the next call merely a setup or a genuine plea for help?

Adam's mission is to offer help and hope, through his speaking engagements and inspirational books, to those who walk the thin blue line.

Adam is truly poised to become the go-to voice of encouragement for officers seeking reassurance from someone who understands what they live every day. The uncertainty they face can also take its toll at home with family, and most importantly, in marriage relationships. In 2000, Adam married his high school sweetheart, but it wasn't a love story without challenges and heartache.

If you ask his friends and family, most will tell you Adam is passionate about his faith, family, and his divine purpose. His most prized role is that of husband to Amber and father to three precious children.

To learn more, you can visit www.TheAdamDavis.com. or Facebook@TheAdamDavis.

Lt. Col. Dave Grossman

A retired US Army Lieutenant Colonel, Dave Grossman is an internationally recognized scholar, author, and speaker who is one of the world's foremost experts in the field of human aggression and the roots of violence and violent crime. He is also one of the nation's leading law enforcement trainers. Dave is a former Army Ranger, West Point psychology professor, and professor of military science who drew on his combined experience to establish a new field of scientific endeavor that he has named Killology. He has served as an expert witness and consultant in numerous federal and state courts, including the *United States vs. Timothy McVeigh*.

Dave has five patents to his name, has published four novels, two children's books, and six nonfiction books, which include his "perennial bestseller" *On Killing* (with over half a million copies sold), and the *New York Times* best-selling book *Control: Exposing the Truth about Guns*, coauthored with Glenn Beck. Some of his other books are *On Combat, Assassination Generation*, and *Sheepdogs: Meet Our Nation's Warriors*, written with Stephanie Rogish.

Acknowledgments from Adam and Dave

To our wives and families, thank you
for your selfless sacrifices while we worked on this book.

To our friends, prayer warriors, and to the Behind the Badge prayer team,
we are deeply grateful for your unwavering support.

To Cyndi Doyle, thank you for your friendship and guidance.

To the BroadStreet Publishing team, this project would not be possible
without your support. You make our work shine and play such
an important role in helping us get this message out.